BLUEPRINT
for a
SPACEFARING
CIVILIZATION

*The Science
of Volition*

JOHN DEMING
with Mike Hamel

Blueprint for a Spacefaring Civilization: The Science of Volition

Copyright © 2025 John Deming

Published by EMT Communications
Colorado Springs, CO 80923
emtcom@comcast.net

ISBN: 979-8-9913245-1-9

Cover and Interior design: Beryl Glass
Cover photo: Shutterstock
First printing — January 2025
Printed in the United States of America

DEDICATION

To my father, John W. Deming, MD, who came from a small Alabama town to become the most well-educated man I've ever known. He was a wise, warm, witty man and the best father a boy could have had. He inspired me to pursue the best explanations of ultimate truths in all fields of knowledge and to ignore the people, well-meaning or not, who tried to dissuade me from such a path.

CONTENTS

ACKNOWLEDGMENTS

John Fountain, for introducing me to the ideas of Andrew Galambos and for being my best friend for forty years.

My father, Dr. John W. Deming, from whom I inherited a love of knowledge so deep and fierce that I have spent my life in pursuit of the most important knowledge I could develop or absorb.

Mike Hamel, my editor, without whom I would never have finished the book. If you understood the theory, it's because Mike simplified my prose and added many touches that clarified some of the more controversial passages.

My children, Lhianna, Emily, Laura, and Trey, and their children, all of whom I hope will live as creative, free individuals in the spacefaring civilization of the future.

Frederic Marks, who was my close friend for thirty years until his death interrupted our warm, creative friendship. Fred inspired me to write the book after he created the first comprehensive explanation of Galambos's ideas on his website: Capitalism, the Liberal Revolution.

Jay Snelson, who first explained scientific epistemology and volitional theory to me in his brilliant course on Galambos's ideas called the V-50 Lectures. Jay had the rare talent of making a lecture on epistemology or volitional theory so entertaining that I was disappointed when it ended.

Kristen Carlson, my closest friend and intellectual companion for over twenty years. I could not have written this book without the vigorous conversations Kris and I enjoyed as young men on fire with the pursuit of knowledge as well as the collaborative writing that flowed therefrom.

John Richard Boren, who would not let me not write this book. He has been a constant source of encouragement once I began writing in earnest. His suggestions made my explanations clearer and more logically consistent.

My sisters, Cathy and Bebe, for always being there for me in my darkest hours. I can't think of two better companions to have as lifelong friends. Their wisdom and measured empathy are rare qualities in today's world.

My high school girlfriend, Nancy Crowell, who saved my life when it was going off the rails at age sixteen. She has a heart bigger than the Andromeda Galaxy.

Carly Taylor Rosenblatt has been my boon companion these past few years. She constantly encouraged me to write this book when I felt overwhelmed. She buoyed my spirit in long conversations full of light and laughter. More than anything, Carly has shown me that a rich platonic friendship between a man and a woman is not only possible but a thing of utter delight.

PREFACE

The science of volition is a revolutionary approach to the social domain that grew out of the intellectual flowstreams of physical science, classical liberalism, and Austrian economics. The late Hungarian American astrophysicist Andrew Galambos and his associates developed the original version of volitional science from 1955 to 1970.[1]

In the 1950s, Galambos worked as a mathematical physicist in the rocket industry of Southern California. He had a dream of private space exploration, but aerospace companies of that era were too busy building intercontinental ballistic missiles with nuclear warheads to be interested in such things. Exploring space on a profit-seeking basis? Are you some kind of nut?

With his background in physics and an intensely curious mind, Galambos reacted by asking: "What social order would channel science into peaceful applications such as space exploration rather than building weapons of war?" He combined his deep knowledge of physics and science with the work of Ludwig von Mises to come up with an answer by creating the original basis of a science of volition.

Galambos founded the Free Enterprise Institute (FEI),[2] where I took courses by him and Jay Snelson from 1975 to 1980, including his yearlong course in physics. I spent the subsequent thirty years pursuing three main fields of study: (1) the development of liberal social theory from Thales and Aristotle to the present, (2) epistemology, and (3) the history of scientific innovation from classical Greece to the present.

I'd started down the path leading to those studies around age fifteen when I realized the adults running the world had no idea what they were doing. I could see we were on a road that would end in the destruction of civilized life. I began questioning everything. Why would an intelligent species apply physical science to build weapons of mass destruction? If the purpose of the Declaration of Independence and the US Constitution was to create a country that protected personal freedom, why was slavery legal until 1865? Why was it deemed acceptable for the US military to forcibly send me and other young men overseas to kill people who posed no discernable threat to us? (I evaded my kidnappers by luck and guile and thus escaped the killing fields of Vietnam.) Why was America involved in a continuous series of wars all over the globe? Whenever I pursued political solutions to these problems, I felt like I'd gone down the proverbial rabbit hole.

Like many young people at the time, I began my intellectual life as a left-wing anti-capitalist, but the more I looked into it, the more disillusioned I became with political solutions. Several years later, I discovered the reason for my disillusionment. Almost everyone believes a political state is necessary to uphold the order that underlies an advanced civilization. The problem is states never achieve the promised results. "Political solution" is an oxymoron. Politics is today's version of alchemy or witchcraft. I sought answers elsewhere and spent years chasing down one false lead after another. Then, one bright spring day in my early twenties, sitting on a Scottish hillside overlooking a dazzling display of sunlight on the surface of the North Sea, I began rethinking my life. I came to the startling conclusion that almost everything I believed was wrong. Thus was born the Blank Slate Principle.

That led to what seemed at the time a mischievous desire. Maybe that made it more enticing. I suddenly wanted to understand two things I had hitherto considered the cause of humanity's problems: physical science and capitalism. I'd accepted that opinion without serious thought. It was the popular zeitgeist of rebellious youth. Scientists had produced nuclear weapons threatening our future. Capitalist corporations were creating environmental havoc.

Still, I had to admit that science and capitalism did deliver the goods. When I thought about it, I realized profit-seeking companies were the source of all the products—clothes, cars, toothpaste, computers, electrical current, etc.—that helped me and everyone else get through the day. So, I wiped my mental slate clean and embarked on a serious study of both subjects. I expected to discover why they were not only wrong but morally repulsive. Then, a funny thing happened. When I uncovered the secret of their success, my objections began to melt away. I experienced the thrill of discovery. I was brimming with excitement at learning how to think scientifically. The secret, I learned, is that science and free market capitalism depend on voluntary interactions. In contrast, the political world depends on coercion. These realizations electrified me. They were observably true and logically valid.

What I share in this book is my version of a science originating in the innovations and strategic insights of Andrew Galambos. Four decades of study after I left his institute led me to develop improvements and incorporate the insights of other social theorists such as Carl Menger, Ludwig von Mises, and F. A. Hayek and evolutionary theorists and epistemologists such as Richard Dawkins, Donald Campbell, and Karl Popper. But it was Galambos who made the crucial counterintuitive breakthroughs that turned liberal social theory into a valid science. For example, he developed:

- An integrated logical structure for volitional science that includes semantically precise definitions for important terms such as *freedom, coercion, morality, justice, property,* and *state*
- A scientifically rigorous concept of absolute morality
- The theory of primary (intellectual) property
- A general theory of production
- Detailed examples of how networked entrepreneurial companies could provide the functions in a free civilization that most people believe only the state can provide

Everyone is fallible, even the greatest scientific minds. We use the knowledge they develop, add to it, and integrate it with the work of others to produce even better explanations. As with other major innovators, Galambos's explanations opened a new path of scientific exploration, showing the way to a civilization of freedom, innovation, and entrepreneurial exploration that can last as long as the universe.

This book is my attempt to explain the science of volition to visionaries who can grasp its revolutionary principles and possess the courage to undertake them.

INTRODUCTION

If you give me several hours of your valuable time, I will give you a revolutionary new way of looking at the world: past, present, and future. It's called volitional science. Among other things, it explains:

- The reason past societies have failed, and current societies are failing
- Why fully free markets are the only social system capable of supporting progress
- How to register, protect, and license intellectual property rights in ways that will accelerate scientific and technological innovation
- A way to value and monetize all forms of property leading to fair compensation that rises with the property's value without an upper limit in time or amount
- How to set in motion an evolutionary market to gradually replace the political state with noncoercive governance
- The minimal conditions necessary to create a lasting society that can become a spacefaring civilization

In these pages, I will explain a new science of the social world. It's called volitional science to distinguish it from the social and political "sciences" taught in today's universities. The latter claim the mantle of science while producing solutions that rely on coercion, never achieve the intended results, and lead to death and destruction on a massive scale.

Volitional science was originally developed by astrophysicist Andrew Galambos and other scientific thinkers in the decades following World War II when they realized humanity faced an unprecedented crisis. We had developed the physical science to produce weapons of mass destruction but had not developed a social science that explained how to prevent their use. Galambos called this historical point the Critical Juncture. Every intelligent species that arises anywhere in the universe will have to deal with and resolve it at some point if they are to survive.

Humanity reached that crossroads on July 16, 1945, when physicists led by J. Robert Oppenheimer exploded the first atomic bomb on the Jornada del Muerto (Journey of Death) desert in New Mexico. Less than a month later, the US military detonated nuclear bombs over the Japanese cities of Hiroshima and Nagasaki, killing around a quarter of a million people, mostly civilians. Today, at least nine nation-states possess such weapons. As of March 2024, there were an estimated 12,000-plus nuclear warheads in their combined arsenals, with enough firepower to destroy civilization many times over. This book deals with how to prevent their use forever.[1]

Volitional science integrates the seminal work of Austrian economists Carl Menger, Ludwig von Mises, and F. A. Hayek with the evolutionary theories of Charles Darwin, Alfred Russel Wallace, Richard Dawkins, et al., and the volitional theory of Andrew Galambos. It is the intellectual culmination of a tradition of liberal thinkers that began in classical Athens and reemerged to flower in the eighteenth-century European Enlightenment. Its target audience is anyone interested in scientific explanations of natural phenomena. It specifically aims at scientific and technical innovators and the entrepreneurs who turn their innovations into products and services.

This book shows that if we continue to develop the science of volition and apply it to create new entrepreneurial communities, humanity can evolve beyond political barbarism into a free, prosperous civilization that expands into the cosmos. It is the only way we will survive the inevitable collapse of political systems.

I will explain volitional science from its foundation to future applications that can give rise to a spacefaring civilization. In the first two chapters, I give an overview of volitional science and define its key terms. Every useful science is built on precise definitions. Chapters 3 and 4 detail the governing societal rules of volitional science, which are based on the ideas of absolute morality and property rights. The two postulates of volitional science are defined and defended:

First Postulate: Volitional beings act to pursue greater happiness. Happiness is subjective to each separate individual.

Second Postulate: All pursuits of happiness that do not involve coercion are equally valid.

The physical, biological, and social contexts in which volitional science operates are dealt with in chapters 5 and 6. They focus on the impact of entropy and evolution in all three realms and provide the context for a deeper understanding of free markets and political states and their different long-term effects on civilizational progress. They examine the similarities and differences between biological and cultural evolution, the main difference being the role played by volitional beings—us.

Chapters 7, 8, and 9 are the book's beating heart. They show how innovators, entrepreneurs, and capitalists can apply volitional science to transform the world. These chapters will disclose exciting new ideas and approaches that include:

- A new theory of compensation
- The Natural Estate
- Natural Estate Trust Companies (NETCO)
- Automatic Remoteness Dilution (ARD)
- Negotiated Remoteness Dilution (NRD)
- Revenue and equity shares
- The open-end concept for setting the financial value of ideas and innovations
- The end of employers and employees

Whereas most socioeconomic theories don't get into the nitty-gritty of how they might be applied in the real world, volitional science offers a detailed blueprint for how to build a spacefaring civilization, which is the subject of chapter 10.

This book isn't for everyone. It's for the few who can understand and apply its ideas to change the world. If that's you, we need your leadership. The path forward will require courage and commitment, and the outcome is uncertain. We have the ability to destroy ourselves and the opportunity to

evolve beyond coercive political states into a spacefaring civilization of perpetual progress. The science of volition offers a
road map to such a future.

Lead on!

1

The Continuing Revolution

Welcome to the continuing revolution. We have only one revolution to offer—just one—for now and forever. That revolution began thousands of years ago when man first crawled out of the cave. Every productive, creative person who's ever lived has added to it. People are adding to it right now. The theory of primary property is the finishing touch to get mankind out of barbarism, a condition of almost certain non-survival, and into total survival capability. The revolution will free us from our vulnerability to the externalities of the universe and the internalities of our own stupidity. It will enable us to develop a civilization in which humans become self-directed evolutionary beings.

—Andrew Galambos

THE SCIENCE OF VOLITION originated in the mind of astrophysicist Andrew Galambos when he realized the advent of nuclear and other weapons of mass destruction

(WMDs) threatened our civilization. He realized we needed a revolutionary approach to the social domain that applied the scientific method to the characteristics of the human social domain. Volitional science shows how we can evolve beyond our current political society of war, violence, and cycles of economic boom and bust into an enduring civilization of peace, freedom, and dynamic stabilized growth. It is part of humankind's continuing revolution from the cave to the stars.

A **volitional being** is a living organism composed of a hierarchy of physical (biochemical) systems. Humans are volitional beings. What differentiates us from all other biological and physical entities and requires a new logical category is the emergence of a new kind of intelligence: the ability to apply reason to make intentional choices in pursuit of a person's unique vision of happiness.

Volitional intelligence is the ability to acquire and use knowledge and reason to make choices in the pursuit of survival and happiness. It's how individuals decide on and commit to a course of action they believe to be in their best interest. Atoms and electromagnetic fields cannot choose to pursue one goal instead of another or change their minds. Mere physical entities have no mind to change. Even the most advanced primates don't possess the intelligence necessary for true volitional action. Their choices are limited to a genetically encoded range of instinctual behaviors.[1]

People have asked me how to tell if a species is volitional. There are two observable markers that provide dispositive evidence a species possesses volitional intelligence: tool-making and symbolic language. Both are evidence of culture.

Thus, if a species makes tools and passes technical knowledge of how to do so to their progeny, resulting in better tools from one generation to the next, that species is volitional. A second, more significant marker for volition would be a symbolic language. Once a species expresses a symbolic language in durable media, it can accumulate knowledge and improve it over time. No animal does either of these things. None has the potential of ever doing so absent millions of years of further Darwinian evolution. Thus, if we discover beings who have developed either of these, it means we've found a new volitional species with whom we can interact and learn from.

Volitional science posits that volitional beings are not mere biological creatures but constitute a new category of being that can arise from Darwinian evolution anywhere life exists in the universe. The two domains of more complex phenomena emerging from the physical world on our planet—the biosphere of living organisms and the social world of volitional beings—are governed by two different but overlapping evolutionary systems: one biological, the other cultural. Once an intelligent species has developed a system of sustained scientific and economic progress, cultural evolution will sooner or later lead to the discovery of knowledge that will allow us to subsume and control, to one degree or another, both the biological and physical worlds.

The current revolution in biological science is at a primitive stage, but it is already producing knowledge leading to cures for some of our most dreaded diseases. If not short-circuited by political interference, the revolution in biology will inexorably extend the human health span and lead to a growing ability to control all aspects of the living world. A few physicists, e.g., Eric Chaisson and Lee Smolin, have speculated the physical universe may also be evolving.[2] If so, it is evolving at a rate too slow for human cognition to notice. We can assume the underlying physical domain is invariant and orderly, thus comprehensible. That assumption underlies the success of physical science.

Volitional Actions

Volitional actions are the fundamental phenomenon upon which volitional science is based. Every time a volitional being acts, he[3] is choosing what he thinks will achieve his ends and, thus, a state of greater satisfaction. In today's interconnected global society, eight billion people are continuously making choices affecting everyone else's choices, resulting in the emergent order we call society.

Society emerges from the interaction of many people choosing various ways to pursue greater satisfaction. The most effective way is mutually profitable cooperation, with people choosing to work with others to better reach their goals. That's the fundamental interaction from which markets develop, giving rise to social systems of peace, prosperity, and progress.

Physical science became a sustained knowledge-generating system when a few seventeenth-century thinkers developed mechanistic explanations of the physical world devoid of anthropomorphism (attributing human traits and purposes to inanimate objects or resorting to mythical human-like gods to describe the causes of natural phenomena). For instance, Galileo and Newton explained oceanic tides not as an effect of Poseidon's whims but as an effect of deterministic natural laws: the interacting gravitational force of the moon and Earth in concert with the Earth's axial rotation. The success of physics made all previous physical explanations obsolete.

Physical science provides an increasingly useful account of the universe, the deterministic context for volitional action. However, physics alone cannot satisfactorily explain biological evolution, much less how societies originate from individual actions and spontaneously enter an orderly, open-ended process of cultural evolution.

History shows most societies have exhibited little or no progress. Poverty and stagnation are the norm. The few that have generated some sustained progress have all eventually disappeared. Volitional science discloses a new, theoretically rigorous category of social order that can prevent such collapses and protect the dynamic internal order necessary for a civilization to expand into the cosmos forever.

The nature of volitional action implies we cannot predict with certainty the outcome of individual actions, much less those of complex social systems, in the exacting way we can predict the future state of physical systems. Yet once we understand the underlying constraints the universe imposes on the world of volitional interactions, we can develop social systems that reliably prevent disastrous societal outcomes and move toward peaceful innovation in a civilization of stabilized durable growth.

Every volitional action involves choosing a means by which someone can best gain what he believes will be a more satisfactory end. No electron, photon, atom, molecule, rock, planet, star, electromagnetic field, oak tree, rhinoceros, mouse, or bacterium pursues happiness in that manner. Humans are the only animals who:

- Create abstract knowledge
- Develop tools and knowledge they pass on to future generations for continual improvement
- Figure out how to learn from their mistakes
- Experience romantic love
- Act hypocritically
- Develop ethical systems
- Write symphonies
- Adjust their behavior to mores of decency concerning sex and defecation

Only volitional beings create culture. Humans dominate our planet because we evolved a unique, more powerful form of thinking that enabled market cooperation whose logistical chains span today's world.

Market: A natural evolutionary social order emerging from noncoercive (voluntary) interactions. A market is the only social order capable of open-ended stabilized growth that can last indefinitely.

Markets derive from noncoercive exchanges to form unrestricted networks based on individuals and their actions. Every meaningful innovation begins in the mind of one person. From there, it can spread wherever there are free markets. An innovation will become a permanent part of the culture if enough people find it valuable. Successful cultures are those with sufficient freedom to allow and quickly adopt innovations.

Ignorance, Uncertainty, and Risk

One of the defining characteristics of volitional beings is an awareness of our ignorance. We realize our knowledge of the world is limited and uncertain. Every action we take is shrouded in a degree of doubt. We can reduce uncertainty by acquiring new information, but we can never eliminate it entirely. Omniscience is given to no one. Civilization is a discovery procedure.

Thus, risk is another universal characteristic of human action. The best way to mitigate risk is to ensure that those responsible for all critical economic functions (1) earn their positions through voluntary market means and (2) have skin in the game. Volitional theory explains how it can be done.

Ignorance, uncertainty, and risk are universal characteristics of volitional action and indispensable components of intelligence. Awareness of our ignorance and the risks associated with acting under uncertainty gives purpose to our lives. It motivated our hominid ancestors to develop the first tools, which sparked the first phase of cultural evolution. An awareness of ignorance led a few unusually curious men to create the explanations we call scientific. When humans began integrating such explanations into a systemic understanding of natural phenomena, we developed the incipient intellectual framework for a civilization of sustained progress. Scientific explanations form a platform of understanding shared by all ethnic groups, genders, and nationalities. Anyone can become a scientist regardless of gender, ethnicity, etc. The only requirement is the ability to produce valuable new explanations of some aspect of our world.

We are not mere collections of atoms reacting mechanistically to physical forces, nor mere animals responding to events with an innate, prespecified range of behavior. We are volitional beings capable of reason and purposeful action. While we are biological organisms whose actions are influenced and often frustrated by somatically encoded instincts, we are the only organisms that, within limits, can choose to control and direct such impulses. Every time a human acts, he attempts to create a better future for himself. In so doing, each person participates in creating the future for all. The most important aspect of human intelligence is the ability to cooperate to better pursue personal ends.

How can we tell if an action or series of actions will have a positive or negative effect? Volitional science answers that question with a principle anyone can understand. It's a universal version of the Hippocratic Oath: "First, do no harm," which principle derives from the idea of absolute, universal morality (discussed in chapter 3).

Volitional science reveals the universal reason all prior civilizations have collapsed and all current societies are collapsing. It explains why no conceivable political system can succeed in the long run. Politics is an error we must scrap if we are to survive. We cannot predict when or how a political system will collapse, but we can predict with a high level of certainty it will. All prior political cultures, even the most successful, have perished. The good news is that once we understand why political governments fail, we can develop realistic alternatives that can prevent such disasters.

Volitional science reveals a realistic, positive alternative to the political state. It shows how we can abandon political barbarism and evolve new forms of *noncoercive* government. Most of these forms already exist in a germinal condition, waiting for visionary entrepreneurs to bring them to fruition.

Scientific Epistemology

I will use a new scientific epistemology to explain how to make society impervious to systemic failure. One reason for the failure of the social sciences thus far is their practitioners have applied the methods of physical science without adapting them to the unique characteristics of the volitional world. They analyze human behavior and social systems as if they were inanimate physical phenomena. I call that "physics envy." They want a science as predictable as physics made up of mathematical formulas. Galambos was a physicist in the aerospace industry. He realized that any valid science of the social domain had to acknowledge the primacy of volition, a quality outside the purview of physics.

Some thoughtful people in the scientific community insist that consciousness, purposeful action, and choice are illusions. They further claim that the only realistic way to explain human behavior is to reduce it to mechanistic physical processes. They imply we are ersatz robots encoded with an illusory belief that we exercise conscious control over our actions. But no one has yet explained how the physical substrate of our neurological system generates someone's unique thoughts, ideas, value judgments, and actions. In the words of Ludwig von Mises: "This ignorance splits the realm of knowledge into two separate fields, the realm of external events, commonly called nature, and the realm of human thought and action."[4] Humans are part of nature. But we have the unique ability to stand outside of nature and explain it.

Physical phenomena exhibit invariant functional relationships that can be expressed in precise mathematical equations. We use such knowledge to build factories that produce airplanes, computers, power-generating plants, and electrical distribution systems. Such products (factories, machines, etc.) work because invariant cause-effect relationships govern the physical world. Physical phenomena do not deviate from the laws of nature. If we observe physical processes that seem to violate a theory of physics or chemistry, it signals the theory is wrong and must be corrected.

When we use probability and statistics to explain reality, such as in quantum physics, it means we're at the frontier of knowledge. Someday, we'll develop more useful explanations of the quantum world, allowing us to better predict events in the microworld. Yet, we will never be able to predict the future of civilizations to a similar degree of accuracy. Societies are not machines that produce specific outcomes as a function of specific inputs. Societies arise from individual interactions, the outcomes of which are never certain.

Cultural evolution is open-ended, yet, like physical and biological evolution, it is subject to underlying universal constraints. Once we understand those constraints, we can apply them to induce cultural evolution that becomes stabilized and impervious to systemic failure.

To develop useful knowledge, we must adapt our methods to the specific characteristics of the subject matter being discussed. Austrian social theorist Carl Menger realized a proper socioeconomic analysis must begin with "the simplest elements that can still be subjected to accurate observation."[5] Thus, we start with individuals and investigate how more complex economic and social phenomena arise from their actions.

Cooperation on the widest possible scale is the great means by which we create, and gain access to, the products and services that improve our lives. We cooperate because it enhances our ability to pursue happiness. Social order emerges from individual interactions, not the other way around. The things we depend on for everyday survival are produced in a global system of cooperative markets. Volitional science explains how markets arise spontaneously from voluntary personal interactions. It reveals the one attribute necessary for them to evolve into durable autonomous systems that, per Scottish philosopher Adam Ferguson, no one planned or designed.[6]

The developers of today's social sciences ignored the groundbreaking epistemological innovations of Menger, Mises, and Hayek. Instead, they crudely applied the methodology of physics to explain the social world, which led them to base their analyses on collectives, not on individuals pursuing different paths. This error gave rise to centralized systems of social engineering that inhibited progress, caused economic stagnation, and precipitated massive human slaughter when people refused to comply with the engineers' plans. In today's Western democracies, that way of thinking has given rise to laws and regulations of such Ptolemaic complexity that no one, not even the nine justices of the US Supreme Court, agrees on what is legal and what is not. Less than half of Supreme Court decisions are unanimous, and those are the easy ones. In his book *Three Felonies a Day*, Harvey Silverglate shows how the average US professional going about his normal life in a nonviolent manner commits several felonies every day without realizing it.[7]

Menger, Mises, and Hayek gave us a pragmatic epistemology that leads to far better explanations of social dynamics. Future scientists may discover how events in the material subsystems of the brain cause specific thoughts, ideas, value judgments, and actions. Even if we discover such knowledge, volitional science would still be a more useful way to explain social phenomena.

Laws and Constraints

The subjective nature of volitional action does not imply that the social world lacks natural laws and universal constraints. Volitional science explains those constraints and the consequences of violating them. It also explains that the basis of all political systems is a fallacy contradicting the natural laws of volition and even some of the fundamental laws of physics.[8]

While volitional science uses a different methodology from physical science, it is a logically integrated science that explains the social world in universal terms. How can complex social systems springing from the subjective choices of billions of people be explained in such terms? To explain, we will draw from an intellectual tradition that began in antiquity, flowered in the Classical Era (from the eighth century BCE to the fifth century CE), and took on its modern form in the first decades of the eighteenth century with the London publication of Bernard Mandeville's poem *The Fable of the Bees*.[9]

Mandeville's subversive yet witty and insightful little book influenced a series of Scottish thinkers, including David Hume, Adam Smith, and Adam Ferguson, to evaluate societies as evolutionary systems that arise from individuals pursuing their own ends. In essence, they were the original complex systems theorists. In 1767, Ferguson identified a new category of natural phenomena: evolutionary social orders resulting from human action but not human design.[10] Examples are language, English common law, science, mathematics, art, music, and markets. Try to design such systems beforehand and you will fail. That doesn't mean we can't understand and develop social structures, including rules of personal behavior that will allow us to flourish and experience sustained progress. It simply means we ground our analysis in individual action and explain how social systems emerge therefrom. What results is an ironic conclusion. A social system of stabilized, open-ended growth requires that we optimize and protect an individual's freedom to pursue whatever path suits his subjective vision of happiness.

As volitional beings, we can do many things that violate the natural laws of volition. But when we do, we will not get the results intended. Coercion, particularly institutional coercion, obstructs the timely recognition of error and inhibits our ability to learn from our mistakes. In a domain as complex as human society, it is virtually impossible to tease out why a society fails or succeeds from empirical data alone. That's why volitional science is a logical science whose insights ultimately derive from the two postulates (see chapter 4) but whose explanations must accord with *observable* results.

When you don't correct policy errors deriving from political laws immediately and locally, they propagate in destructive ways. Coercion suppresses and often prohibits error correction, something markets do naturally, quickly, and continuously. When error is imposed on an entire society by a central authority, it has rapidly destroyed civilizations that have endured for centuries.

Until we understand the natural laws, regularities, and constraints governing human action, we will continue to let ignorant political demagogues pile one mistake on top of another in a desperate attempt to fix earlier blunders. This compounds errors that, sooner or later, result in large-scale disasters. Our world could not survive without its highly technical infrastructure. Bridges, roads, electrical grids, telecom systems, and water purification plants must be maintained and upgraded. Without a deeper understanding of social systems, particularly regarding the efficacy of markets over political systems, we will face infrastructure breakdowns that threaten our survival.

People have sought peace, prosperity, and freedom for thousands of years but have produced the opposite. Prior major cultures like sixth-century BCE Persia, classical Athens and Rome, and China during the Song dynasties (960–1279) all collapsed because their members did not understand the cause of social, economic, and political failure. More importantly, they did not grasp the societal conditions necessary for sustained progress. Every current political system exhibits the characteristics that have always preceded social collapse. Isn't it about time we try something new?

There is much to be learned from the single spectacular exception to the sad history of societal failures. Something happened in sixteenth- and seventeenth-century Europe, giving rise to more than four hundred years of *sustained* progress. Volitional science explains why science developed in Europe, why Newtonian science is the foundation of that progress, and how we can apply the knowledge gained from that analysis to develop a lasting civilization through a peaceful entrepreneurial process that has the side benefit of expanding and strengthening individual liberty.

Open-Ended Systems

Markets are open-ended social systems capable of unlimited growth. There is no predetermined teleological end-state or nirvana toward which we are heading, as posited by Marx and other socialists. End-states imply stagnation and death. In sharp contrast, markets allow for an unlimited number of potential pathways into an open-ended future. If we develop such durable markets, we will never reach an end-state. Acquirable knowledge is infinite. Civilization is a discovery procedure.[11] Progress in all dimensions of existence is potentially infinite. In the words of physicist David Deutsch, "We are always near the beginning of infinity."[12]

We have developed powerful explanations of physical and biological phenomena. We have now produced explanations of similar power for the socioeconomic domain. But this knowledge is still virtually unknown, if not ignored, by most. For instance, we now understand how markets are governed and stabilized by internal feedback from proprietary incentives deriving from property ownership. As Mises and Hayek have shown, a technologically progressive economy cannot exist without the information conveyed by price signals that emerge from transactions based on strong property rights.[13]

Yet our current, pre-volitional theory understanding of markets is insufficient to produce a durable liberal civilization. Except for the brilliant but little-known nineteenth-century American Lysander Spooner, no one until Galambos understood how to integrate scientific innovation into markets via intellectual property ownership. Volitional science holds that when society accepts that innovators own the ideas they create, it will give rise to market incentives, making it profitable to build proprietary systems to protect and compensate them for the value their ideas generate. If you think of the term *compensation*, it's not difficult to grasp that compensating people for the value of their work is an important component of justice. It's also something markets do so naturally and effectively that it will entirely replace the state and its defective patent and copyright system.

Volitional science and its derivative ideas will only be taken up and applied if innovators and entrepreneurs find it profitable. Unlike every other social theory I'm aware of, in volitional science, the means fit the ends. Since the civilization it proposes is based on the principle of noncoercion, the means used to achieve it are also noncoercive.

Innovation and Freedom

To evolve into a spacefaring civilization, we do not have to elect the right people to political office, educate the public, or foment a rebellion to replace one set of rulers with another. We only have to motivate a small number of people to make the needed changes. Lasting cultural revolutions always follow the same pattern. Innovation comes into the world beneath the notice of almost everyone. Someone conceives a powerful new idea and discloses it to the few people who might understand it.

The spread of innovation is not planned or directed by a central authority. If anything, central authorities act to suppress conceptual breakthroughs, which they view as threats to their power. Yet, given a sufficient degree of freedom, innovation finds its way into new products and services via the most powerful transmission system in the world: entrepreneurs operating in free markets.

In its early stages, innovation seems to gain traction too slowly to make a lasting difference. Its effects never happen overnight. For example, in 1865, Cambridge physicist James Clerk Maxwell disclosed four equations predicting the existence of electromagnetic waves. He published a refined version in 1872. In 1889, Heinrich Hertz, at the Technische Hochschule in Karlsruhe, Germany, confirmed the existence of such waves by transmitting and receiving them over twelve meters in his laboratory. But even Hertz did not realize the importance of what he had done. One of his students asked how this miracle could be applied. "It's of no use whatsoever," Hertz answered. "This is just an experiment that proves Maestro Maxwell was right, we just have these mysterious electromagnetic waves we cannot see with the naked eye. But they are there."[14]

"So, what next?" asked the student.

Hertz shrugged. "Nothing, I guess."

Yet only a few years later, the English physicist Oliver Heaviside said, "Three years ago, electromagnetic waves were nowhere. Shortly afterward, they are everywhere."[15] By 1897, Marconi and Tesla, backed by private capital, were sending and receiving radio waves over distances as long as ten kilometers. In 1901, Marconi transmitted the first transatlantic wireless telegraph. In the early twenty-first century, the global system connecting everyone instantaneously via the internet, cloud, mobile phones, and laptops is downstream of Maxwell's innovation.

Another powerful example of lasting revolutionary change occurred in the seventeenth century. On 17 February in the year 1600, Giordano Bruno was burned at the stake in the Campo de Fiori in Rome. His crime was to promulgate such wild ideas as Copernicus's heliocentric hypothesis and his own notion that the sun was a star, one of innumerable stars in a universe with no fixed center. He intuited those ideas for which he had no clear evidence other than his rational mind. Since those insights turned out to be right, I consider Bruno a scientist of the highest importance.

Then, in 1633, the Catholic Inquisition placed Galileo under house arrest until his death in 1642 for his sly advocacy of heliocentrism and other heresies in his immensely popular *Dialogue Concerning the Two Chief World Systems*.[16] In 1687, less than a century after Bruno's execution and only fifty years after Galileo was found guilty of heresy, Isaac Newton published the *Principia Mathematica*. Within several decades of its publication, virtually every educated person in the Western world accepted Newtonian science and a heliocentric planetary system with elliptical orbits as their worldview.

What followed was a flowering of intellectual freedom known as the Enlightenment, which, in turn, led to the American Revolution, the Industrial Revolution, and today's high standard of living. Thus, the most consequential ideological revolution in history happened within a century of Bruno's execution when the most influential European intellectuals had adopted Newtonian science as their worldview. That occurred at a time when the most advanced form of communication was the delivery of letters and books by sailing ships and horses. Today's global telecommunication system means a new revolution in human thought could happen far more rapidly.

As scientists and engineers understand the significance of what innovators have wrought, and as entrepreneurs grasp the potential for outsized returns from technical applications, innovation bursts forth. It spreads in an evolutionary competition of companies producing products and technical systems that transform entire societies. It happens because, at every stage of dissemination, people pursue profit. This creates momentum that ratchets irreversibly into the future.

With that brief introduction, let's begin exploring the fundamental theory of the science of volition.

★ ★ ★

Recap

- Humans are volitional beings—living organisms composed of a hierarchy of physical (biochemical) systems. Humans possess volitional intelligence, the ability to acquire and use knowledge and reason to make subjective choices in the pursuit of survival and happiness. We decide on and pursue courses of action we believe are in our best interest, something mere biological creatures cannot do.

- Humans make choices to pursue greater satisfaction that affect everyone else's choices, resulting in the order we call society. The most effective societies develop when people work together in markets to achieve their ends.

- Ignorance, uncertainty, and risk are components of volitional intelligence. Awareness of our ignorance and the risks associated with acting under uncertainty gives purpose to our lives. It led curious men to create the explanations we call science, which led to a growing understanding of natural phenomena and the physical world. Volitional science is a logically integrated science explaining the social world in absolute and universal terms. As with the physical sciences, its explanations can be verified by observable results.

- Volitional science reveals why prior civilizations have collapsed and current societies are collapsing. It offers a realistic alternative to the political state and a path toward new forms of noncoercive government. It also shows that the basis of all political systems is a fallacy that contradicts the natural laws of volition and even some of the fundamental laws of physics.

- A market is a natural evolutionary social order rising from spontaneous, noncoercive interactions. Free markets are the only social order capable of unlimited growth that can last indefinitely.

- Volitional science holds that when society accepts that innovators own the ideas they create, it will give rise to market incentives, making it profitable to build proprietary systems to protect, fund, and compensate innovators. Properly compensating inventors and innovators for the value of their work is a major component of justice and something only markets can do naturally and effectively.

2

Semantic
Precision

It can scarcely be denied that the supreme goal of all theory is to make the irreducible basic elements as simple and as few as possible without having to surrender the adequate representation of a single datum of experience.

—Albert Einstein

EVERY USEFUL SCIENCE is built out of precise definitions. The singular purpose of semantic precision is clear communication. It's that simple. Precise definitions preserve semantic accuracy across myriad channels of communication. As long as each party to a conversation defines their terms precisely, they can communicate effectively, even if their definitions are different.

Semantic precision makes innovators' lives more convenient and their work more valuable. Precise definitions accelerate the spread of new ideas while keeping their semantic content unsullied. Scientists eventually converge on the most useful definition for essential terms through a voluntary market dynamic. That's why physicists and chemists have accepted the same definitions for such terms as *force, momentum, mass, valence,* etc. Semantic precision has worked well in the physical sciences and is one of the methodological tools we can apply directly to social theory.

Semantically precise definitions demarcate a clear boundary around each concept, separating it from everything else. Precise definitions follow the principles of set or category theory. Researchers from AI scientist Fei-Fei Li to neuroscientist Raymond Tallis point to categorization as one of the most critical components of human intelligence. It's a necessary step on the road to understanding universal principles and natural laws.

Synonyms in science are rare and tend to be eliminated over time. Scientific terms preserve a unique meaning for each key term across all languages, cultures, and historical eras. That's not to deny that terminology evolves as scientific knowledge grows and adapts to discoveries. As a particular term evolves, it is clarified and made more precise. It may be separated into two or more ideas, but as scientists discuss and clarify new terms, they eventually settle on standard terminology. Yet, it is fascinating how many terms of physical science have retained the same essential meaning for centuries. The key point is that at any time, all scientists use the same key terms to mean one and only one thing, and that's what we do in volitional science. Everyone will know what we mean when we use terms such as *freedom, coercion,* and *justice.*

In addition to being precise and unique, a good definition should be concise. The reason is again straightforward: science is a human endeavor. It is created by people in a cooperative effort to develop better explanations of the world around and within us. The human mind can only deal with so much complexity at any one time. We break down our explanations of complex worlds into simple concepts and link them logically into an explanatory system. We are born with a powerful logical operator that evolved as an essential component of volitional intelligence. It allows us to organize the key terms of knowledge in ways that are easy to deal with. We don't have to remember everything. We can start with simple premises and reach useful conclusions by following a chain of logic derived from the premises.

Complex definitions are unusable. If every time we come across a term, we have to recall several pages of a definition that includes terms with similarly complex definitions, we won't use it. Simple definitions of fundamental ideas have always gained acceptance over more complex definitions. It's a corollary of Occam's Razor.[1]

Scientific definitions are arbitrary. No committees of high mandarins determine which definitions are acceptable and which are not. Newton's terms and definitions gained acceptance because other thinkers found his definitions more useful than competing ones, e.g., those developed by Descartes in his notion of Cartesian vortices.[2]

Definitions are the nodes of knowledge. Concise definitions make the organization of scientific knowledge more convenient. Simple does not imply good or better in some ultimate sense. Einstein's quote at the beginning of the chapter gives a useful standard for judging the definitions of science.

Science is an evolutionary market in ideas. Thus, while Newton's successors used his explanations and terminology, they did not shy away from improving or adapting them to discoveries such as electromagnetic waves. Definitions become important through others' use of them. The more an idea or definition is accepted, developed, and applied, the more important it becomes. **Importance** is a measure of the total amount of people and property something affects over time.

Definitions are made up of words that have already been defined. The meanings of these other words are also built out of words that must be defined. Do you see the problem? If definitions are made up of words made up of words, where does it all begin? The answer in science is the operational definition.

Operational Definitions

An **operational definition** defines a term by specifying the method of determining or measuring whatever is being defined. Mass, length, and time—the fundamental parameters of physics—are defined operationally. There is no alternative. There are no other already-defined terms out of which to construct their definitions. Since mass, length, and time are the concepts of which all physical units of measurement are constructed, if we don't define those terms operationally, we have no physics. Therefore, to develop a cohesive, integrated set of concepts that match the standards of scientific discourse, we must begin with operational definitions. In volitional science, we start with an operational definition of property. I'm using Richard Boren's definition of property because it clarifies Galambos's original definition while preserving its meaning.

Property: Anything created by a volitional being.

The science of volition is based on property—how it is created, controlled, exchanged, and utilized. As such, property is to volitional science as energy is to physics and life to biology. It is the concept around which the entire subject is organized. When we get to the definitions of *own*, *owner*, and *ownership* just ahead, we will see that parents create their children but do not own them. Parents are responsible for their children's safety, health, and education until they are ready to assume adult responsibilities.

Property is everything, tangible and intangible—all the stuff—we create or produce. It is everything that would not exist in a universe devoid of volitional beings. Its creation is the most important aspect of volitional intelligence.

There are three kinds of property: primordial, primary, and secondary.

(1) Primordial property (P0, pronounced "P-zero"): A person's physical body, including his brain and neurological system. It is the unique biophysical system that supports a person's existence as a conscious, volitional being.

Recognizing our body as our physical apparatus is the beginning of self-consciousness and intentional action. We are far more than a physical body, but the body is the observable material marker for ourselves and others of an identifiable, separate self.

> **(2) Primary property (P1):** The intangible derivatives of a person's physical body, including the mind. It includes beliefs, thoughts, ideas, actions, innovations, designs, songs, patterns, stories, and emotions. Other forms of P1 include behaviors, attitudes, perspectives, opinions, agreements, contracts, messages, artistic creations, and relationships with others.

Lysander Spooner's[3] and Andrew Galambos's concept of primary property is similar to, but more comprehensive than, what is today called intellectual property. If we define importance as a measure of the amount of people and property someone's work affects over time, intellectual or intangible property is the most significant property we produce. When P1 ownership is registered, protected, and licensed via noncoercive profit-seeking ventures such that a thriving market in ideas blossoms, it will be an important step in the evolution of humanity into a peaceful entrepreneurial civilization that guarantees our survival.

The owner of primary property cannot transfer ownership to someone else. His creation of the property is an immutable historical fact. An innovator of valuable P1 can, however, license its use via a methodology we explore later in the book. Ownership will not inhibit the free flow of ideas; it will enhance and protect their dissemination in ways you can't yet imagine.

Primary property is the most valuable property as measured through voluntary market transactions. I estimate it makes up 99+ percent of the value of all property. If you think that's exaggerated, consider that all tangible property begins as an idea in someone's mind.

> **(3) Secondary property (P2):** The tangible derivatives of a person's actions, e.g., tables, chairs, refrigerators, airplanes, semiconductors, shoes, automobiles, telephones, houses, pharmaceuticals, etc. An owner can transfer ownership of secondary property by voluntary exchange.

Society and Markets

The generic term for a social collective is *society*. A **society** is an association of individuals interacting to produce and exchange property. To understand a society, let's briefly discuss how and why it arises. Societies appeared when people discovered they could more effectively pursue happiness by cooperating. Cooperation is where two or more people choose to work together to pursue shared or even quite different ends.

A **market** is an open-ended, adaptive evolutionary system of property exchanges. Why do individuals cooperate to create and exchange property? Because they believe it will increase their happiness. There's no other reason. These transactions are potential win-win exchanges. People will only undertake them if they expect to gain from them.

In contrast, political transactions are coercive, thus win-lose. They force people to do things they don't want to do or forbid them from doing what they want to do. If people must be forced to undertake a transaction, it means they prefer not to do it. They believe there are better ways to use available resources to pursue their vision of happiness. Every political action aims, in one way or another, to thwart our pursuit of greater satisfaction. We will only survive and prosper by evolving into a society that fosters win-win exchanges and makes it practically impossible to gain from coercive win-lose exchanges.

Markets provide a stable context where individuals can cooperate in their pursuit of varying goals. Cooperation occurs within families and among people who negotiate contractual terms that govern their interactions. Cooperation has extended over the entire planet via interconnected global networks of explicit and implicit contractual agreements. It's effective because it's voluntary. Forcing someone to cooperate would be an internal contradiction. Forced cooperation is slavery. Any time someone employs coercion to control someone else or his property, the coercer has enslaved that person.

Markets are the most productive social system ever devised because they result from voluntary interactions of individuals, each pursuing his subjective vision of happiness. Markets can only arise from people who feel some degree of security in their property ownership. Markets have an inbuilt system of governance derived from participants' implicit or explicit agreement to respect ownership. All transactions are governed by an understanding that each party is exchanging property they own. For example, you may be a talented designer of advanced microprocessors, which skill you agree to apply to the products of a semiconductor company in exchange for monetary compensation. Your design skills are your property, and the money you're paid derives from company revenues, which belong to the company's owner(s).

Since markets are progressive by nature and knowledge is cumulative, the advantage property ownership has provided to citizens of Western culture would normally accelerate and compound relative to less free cultures. However, Western nation-states have lost much of that advantage by failing to protect property ownership and free markets from political coercion.

Ownership

Every society must address the issue of who controls what property. How it's done will determine, more than anything else, what type of society it will become. In volitional science, ownership derives from the person who created the property.

> **To own:** The right to exercise exclusive control over one's physical body (primordial property) and the primary and secondary property originating from that body. You own your body and everything you create, produce, or acquire in voluntary exchange.

> **Owner:** The person who inhabits and thus owns his physical body (primordial property) and the primary and secondary property he creates or acquires in voluntary exchange.

> **Ownership:** The relationship of exclusive control owners exercise over property they own.

From these definitions, we can see that:

- Volitional beings own themselves.
- You own your mind, thoughts, ideas, actions, and labor.
- You own your mistakes.
- You have ownership rights in all the agreements you negotiate and enter into. When you create agreements and contracts, those are property jointly owned per explicit terms by the parties to the agreement.
- Natural resources, including land, are not property and thus cannot be owned. However, the use of natural resources is property. Anyone who creates access to natural resources, such as uninhabited land, minerals, or crude oil, has created new property, which bestows an exclusive right to control the resources.
- Ownership provides powerful incentives for individuals to engage in productive activities that generate progress. An easy way to gauge a society's capacity to generate progress would be to estimate the amount of capital (property that can be applied to further production) it has accumulated relative to other societies.

Ownership of ideas has long been recognized de facto in science by its naming procedures: Archimedes' law of the lever, Newton's laws of motion, Maxwell's equations, Darwin's (and Wallace's) theory of evolution, Einstein's theory of relativity, Brownian motion, etc. Formalizing the relationship between innovators and their innovations as a property right would be a straightforward, if controversial, step. But it's becoming less controversial as it becomes more obvious to intellectual leaders that a stable market in scientific and technological innovation is the key to progress.

Ancillary Definitions

Other important definitions derive from the definitions of property and ownership:

Interference: Any reduction in an owner's control of his property without the owner's permission.

Coercion: Any attempted intentional interference with the property of an owner without the owner's permission or consent.

Force: Coercion effected through physical violence or the threat of physical violence.

Fraud: Coercion effected through deception.

Contract: An uncoerced agreement between two or more people for the purpose of exchanging property. Contracts set the terms governing cooperative efforts to create new property.

Slavery: The control of a person's property, including their primordial property (physical body), without their permission or consent.

Stealing or theft: Seizure of a person's property without permission or consent.

Crime: A successful act of coercion.

Injustice: A crime to which there is no recourse.

Justice: The absence of injustice.

Liberty: The condition in which an individual has full control of his or her property.

Government: Any profit-seeking entity offering products and services to protect property to which customers may voluntarily subscribe.

Taxation: A euphemism for massive, recurring theft carried out by a small group of people within a society with the tacit approval of most others.

Communism: The abolition of private property.

Civilization: A society where the prevailing commercial and personal customs derive from the principle of noncoercion. It is a society in which respect for property ownership has become customary.

State: An organization that claims and exercises a legal monopoly of coercion within a specified territorial boundary. It is an apparatus of coercion accorded respectability or legitimacy by the public.

State

A **state** is a group of people within a society who use coercion to achieve their ends and whose actions are accepted as legitimate by most people. In contrast, volitional science addresses how we can apply noncoercive means alone to solve the problems people created political states to solve. Whether it is conflict resolution, a basic level of security, crime prevention, or even large-scale territorial defense, means-end analysis reveals that entrepreneurial markets can provide superior solutions in every case.

Political laws and regulations can never solve problems; instead, they will always result in the opposite of what was intended.[4] I arrive at this conclusion without making value judgments or falling into the Manichaean fallacy of accusing anyone of malicious intent. I do not assume people are intrinsically evil. Such assumptions do not lead to solutions. David Deutsch's Principle of Optimism states, "All evils are caused by insufficient knowledge."[5] That's one of the fundamental premises of volitional science: evil is a result of ignorance. I'm not implying we can teach political demagogues or religious terrorists to be nice people. Instead, we apply scientific and entrepreneurial knowledge to build systems that protect property and make it invulnerable to their attacks.

Markets produce an overwhelming technological advantage, making them less vulnerable to aggression from primitive coercive societies. The Allies won WWII because the US and Britain had more productive capitalist economies compared to the more primitive slave societies of Nazi Germany and Imperial Japan. America overwhelmed the Axis powers with high production.

We don't need to get into Manichaean good-guy/bad-guy arguments over values. When one allows one's values and opinions to override reasoned analysis, one has strayed from the path of science. In volitional science, we use means-ends analysis, the logic of choice, and historical facts to show why noncoercion works more effectively than state coercion.

Britain and America preserved a degree of freedom (see definition below) that produced the high standard of living we enjoy today. Unfortunately, the Anglosphere lost the plot in the twentieth century when its leaders adopted political coercion under the banner of socialism as the primary way to solve problems. Consider the words of historian Robert

Higgs, who described the results of state actions during the twentieth century in this way:

> In the past century alone, states have caused hundreds of millions of deaths—not to the combatants of both sides of the many wars they've launched, whose casualties loom very large—but to their own populations, who they have chosen to shoot, bomb, shell, hack, stab, beat, gas, starve, work to death, and otherwise obliterate in ways too grotesque to contemplate calmly. J. R. Rummel, who has spent a lifetime compiling data on political democide (non-war state killing), has a total of 262 million democide victims in the twentieth century.[6]

Higgs then explained that political states are wasteful, clumsy, and inept at almost everything they do, with one exception.

> [States] are exceptionally good at wreaking death and destruction. Indeed, if they were not, they could not sustain themselves as states. In a functional sense, we can define the state as an organization with a comparative advantage in deliberately, violently killing people and appropriating and destroying wealth.[7]

Freedom

Freedom: The societal condition wherein each individual has 100 percent control over his property.

People use the important term *freedom* to mean many different, often conflicting things. Until now, there has been no clear standard definition. Several common meanings of *free* or *freedom* contradict each other. Jean-Jacques Rousseau, Karl Marx, Franklin Roosevelt, Adolf Hitler, and Mao Zedong used the term to mean something different from what it meant to John Locke, David Hume, Thomas Paine, Lysander Spooner, and Andrew Galambos.

Freedom implies the right to do whatever owners want with their property except use it to interfere with another's similar right. It implies a society where one person cannot force his will upon or subjugate another.

Freedom is an ideal standard that can only be approached asymptotically. But when it is carried out through voluntary market ventures, we can get much closer to zero coercion than you may think. Freedom leads to innovation, progress, artistic efflorescence, and prosperity. Innovators can only flourish in freedom. And the greater the degree of freedom, the greater the quality and quantity of innovations. Innovations are the fount of all wealth. If you want a prosperous society at all levels, focus on what leads to greater freedom and leave innovators alone.

The level of freedom in a society is inversely proportional to the coercive power of political and other authorities to control someone's life and property. The most harmful kind of coercion in terms of its long-term negative effects is institutional coercion, particularly political and religious coercion. Its most insidious manifestation is the ability of political agents to suppress innovation by threatening the lives and property of innovators who create and disseminate new ideas. In addition, state regulators interfere with the entrepreneurs who produce and market goods and services in a noncoercive manner. Bureaucrats decrease entrepreneurial profits, which are the source of capital for further innovation. Coercion, particularly state coercion, always undermines production, lays waste to wealth, destroys information, and suppresses innovation. Freedom has the opposite effect.

Matt Ridley gave an excellent example from the recent past.

The incandescent bulb reigned supreme for more than a century, being still the dominant form of lighting, at least in domestic settings, well into the first decade of the twenty-first century. When it gave way to a new technology, it did so under duress. That is to say, it had to be banned, because its replacement was so unpopular. The decision by governments all over the world around 2010, lobbied by the makers of compact fluorescent bulbs, to "phase out" incandescents by fiat in the interest of cutting carbon dioxide emissions, proved to be a foolish one. . . . The cost to Britain alone, of this coerced purchase and the subsidy that accompanied it, has been estimated at about £2.75bn.

Worst of all, had governments waited a few more years, they would have found a far better replacement coming along that was even more frugal in energy and had none of the disadvantages: light-emitting diodes, or LEDs. The reign of the compact fluorescents lasted just six years before they too were rapidly abandoned and manufacturers stopped producing them because of the falling cost and rising quality of LEDs.[8]

In other words, when individuals with political power arbitrarily force a technological solution on an entire culture, they almost never get it right. Market solutions that result from an ongoing process of trial and error by entrepreneurs operating at risk always get it better in the long run. When I say *always*, I mean the word in the sense of reaching the optimal solution at the time, given the level of knowledge and available resources.

Noncoercion

Scientific knowledge grows in an environment of noncoercion. Once a market in ideas gets traction, it will always develop better explanatory knowledge through an iterative cycle of innovation, disclosure, discussion, trial and error, technological application, and acceptance or rejection of the results. Science can develop in a relatively coercive broader society if participants do not allow institutional coercion to seep in and contaminate their interactions.

If the wider society becomes too coercive, scientific progress will wither into Lysenkoist pseudoscience enforced by institutional coercion.[9] That frequently occurs when the state becomes the major source of funds for science. When bureaucrats with no skin in the game control which people and projects get funded, science is infected with the virus of coercion, and progress will slow.

Noncoercion is the key to science. Period. Scientific progress will always result from a strong tradition of noncoercive interactions in the development of knowledge. Without that condition, the development of scientific knowledge will never lead to a better understanding of our world.

As I developed my understanding of these ideas, I stumbled upon a remarkable principle: *coercion always destroys information*. No exceptions. By information, I mean new data at least one person finds useful or valuable. This definition derives from Claude Shannon's mathematical theory of communication.[10] The statement is also true if you substitute the term *knowledge* for *information*.

Freedom and coercion are inversely correlated. Freedom is the absence of coercion. It is an ideal standard but one sufficiently pragmatic to become the governing principle of future civilizations. Even when we consider the malicious and emotionally turbulent nature of the human beast, we will find it surprising how closely we can approach a condition of 100 percent freedom and 0 percent coercion and how pragmatic such a goal is.

★ ★ ★

Recap

- Science is an evolutionary market in ideas. It requires precise definitions to communicate. Definitions are the building blocks of knowledge. Scientists decide on the most useful definition for essential terms through a voluntary market process.
- The key definitions in volitional science are:

- Property: A volitional being's life and all non-procreative derivatives thereof. Volitional science recognizes three forms of property:
  - Primordial property: A person's physical body, including the brain and neurological system.
  - Primary property: The intangible derivatives of a person's physical body and mind, including actions, thoughts, ideas, novels, symphonies, designs, movies, scientific theories, personal diaries, letters, etc.
  - Secondary property: The tangible derivatives of a person's actions.
- Society: An association of individuals interacting to produce and exchange property. People formed societies when they realized they could more effectively pursue happiness *by* cooperating. This led to the development of markets. A market is an open-ended, adaptive system of noncoercive property exchanges.
- Ownership: The relationship of exclusive control owners exercise over their property. Every society must address the issue of who controls what property. How that's done will determine what type of society it becomes. In volitional science, ownership derives from the person who created the property.
- State: An organization exercising a legal monopoly of coercion within a specified territorial boundary. It is an apparatus of coercion accorded legitimacy by the public. In contrast, volitional science addresses how to apply noncoercive means alone to solve the problems people created political states to solve.

- Freedom: The societal condition wherein everyone has 100 percent control over their property. Freedom implies everyone has the right to do whatever they want with their property except use it to interfere with others' similar right to control their property.

- Coercion: Any attempted intentional interference with the property of an owner without the owner's permission or consent. Coercion always destroys information and suppresses knowledge. Noncoercion is the key to progressive science and free markets. To access the fruits of high production, society must act according to the principle of noncoercion, which means respecting owners' rights to control their property.

3

Absolute Morality

Scientific methods are merely ways of rejecting or supporting factual claims that emerge from theories. . . . Facts never lead to actions all by themselves. They can only inform a system of values. I would rather live in a society based on good facts interpreted by a good value system than in any other kind of society.
—David Sloan Wilson

CAN THERE BE A SCIENTIFICALLY VALID universal basis of absolute morality independent of gender, ethnicity, and all religious, political, or cultural preferences? Let's begin with this definition.

Absolute morality: The minimal set of rules governing behavior a volitional species must adopt as customary for its civilization to survive and prosper indefinitely.

Henry Hazlitt put it another way: Absolute morality would be the minimal set of rules leading to cooperation on the widest possible scale. Such morality must have the following attributes:

- It must be a rule or rules of conduct that draw a clear boundary between moral and immoral actions.
- It must be simple enough that everyone can infer how to act within its constraints.
- It must accord with human nature; i.e, it cannot be a set of rules that are too burdensome or impossible to follow.
- It must not put one person's right to a morally valid action in conflict with another's morally valid action.
- It must be general and adaptable enough to apply in every potential interaction between volitional beings.
- It must be a rational concept that does not depend on ideas that cannot be logically or empirically verified.
- It must have the effect of fostering innovation, which is humanity's most effective means of ensuring our survival and prosperity.
- It must support a societal trend that reduces stealing, murder, rape, war, and other coercive acts to zero.
- It must be consistent with the concepts of freedom and progress.[1]

If we can establish that a theory of morality applies to every species of intelligent (volitional) beings everywhere in the universe, with zero exceptions, we can be confident it is a universal law of nature. As with the laws and theories of physics, if people do not act according to a valid moral rule, they will suffer consequences that are the opposite of those intended.

Absolute, Relative, and Universal

The notion of *absolute* may arouse skepticism in thoughtful people when applied to morality. First, some simple definitions:

Absolute: That which is independent of arbitrary standards of determination. It is the same for all observers.

Relative: That which is dependent on an observer's frame of reference.

Universal: A law that applies everywhere in the universe.

A common intellectual fallacy asserts, "There are no absolutes; everything is relative." But the statement itself asserts an absolute that allows no exceptions. It is self-contradictory. When we say something is an absolute, it means we believe we're homing in on a fundamental aspect of the universe. Of course, we may be wrong. In science, when we're wrong, we'll find out.

In the physical domain, pi (π) and the speed of light are examples of absolutes. In the volitional domain, freedom—the societal condition that exists when everyone has full (100 percent) control over their property—is an absolute standard.

It is not a fact like pi or the speed of light, but an ideal standard that allows for no exceptions. It applies to all societies of volitional beings. It is the ideal condition to which a volitional species will aspire if it is to survive and prosper indefinitely.

Absolute does not imply we have reached the end of knowledge or stated the final word on any subject. It bears repeating that acquirable knowledge is infinite. There never will be a final theory of anything or everything. Science is an ongoing process of people discovering and organizing ever-better explanations of natural phenomena. The one thing necessary for continual scientific progress is a social system that protects theoretical innovators and inventors from coercion. The goal is to evolve into a social system that protects everyone from coercion. I emphasize innovators because their mistreatment has harmed the long-term prospects of our civilization far more than the mistreatment of others. When major innovators, the true source of our ability to survive and prosper, are protected from coercion, everyone will be protected. I will explain the basis of that assertion in a later chapter.

One of the salient traits of intelligent beings is our ability to learn and innovate. As we develop a better scientific understanding of human action and the societies that emerge therefrom, we can predict the longer-term consequences of adopting specific social systems in common-sense probabilistic terms. Even better, we can apply volitional science to predict what types of social structure will support our survivability, prosperity, and ability to expand into the cosmos.

In the market of scientific ideas, we can ascertain someone's confidence in an idea, hypothesis, theory, or principle by the risk they assume in using or promulgating it. Entrepreneurs who build technology businesses take a proprietary risk in their entrepreneurial ability and in the validity of the theoretical science underlying the applications they develop. Their success or failure will be recorded by the capital they accrue and their reputation going forward.

Scientists put their reputations at risk every time they disclose a new idea or claim someone else's new idea is a good or better explanation. They produce explanations, discoveries, and inventions. They aim to produce the most useful explanations of whatever phenomena they're addressing. They search for absolutes to explain a world in which everything we observe is relative.

The test of an idea is its voluntary acceptance, rejection, and further development over time. Market acceptance is the great filter of cultural and scientific evolution. Markets are brutally effective at filtering out bad ideas and brilliantly efficient at selecting good ones. An idea will lead to applications that either work or don't work. People risk their reputations every time they accept or reject a new idea. Every heuristic for judging the value of an idea is a short-term, at-risk guess as to its ultimate acceptance.

Isaac Newton established the basis of modern science when he proved mathematically that gravitation is a universal law. Newton showed the gravitational force causing a small stone to fall toward the Earth's surface is the same force binding the planets in elliptical orbits around the sun. When we assume the same attractive force operates throughout the universe in the way Newton and, two centuries later, Einstein did, we find it generates further useful explanations, allowing us to predict everything from the arc of a stone someone hurls to the rotation of galaxies. Before Newton, most educated people assumed the Earth and the heavens were separate realms that operated according to different natural laws. After Newton, we assume the physical universe follows the same laws everywhere.

Scientists search for universals in a world where everything we can observe is relative to our frame of reference. The pursuit of physical, biological, and volitional absolutes assumes that an orderly universe exists independent of our subjective experience and perception. It is everywhere governed by laws we can discover, explain, and apply to useful ends. David Deutsch and Andrew Galambos said the universe is comprehensible, but creating the theoretical explanations that allow us to comprehend it is very difficult. That's why we honor the innovators who successfully do so.

Objective and Subjective

Newtonian science and the four centuries of downstream discoveries it spawned demonstrate the universe is comprehensible. Yet our knowledge of its workings originates in fallible minds that develop explanations out of data constrained by the limitations of our sensory *apparati*. Thus, all knowledge is subjective. Objective knowledge is a chimera. However, the impossibility of objective knowledge does not preclude a world of relations existing outside our subjective experience. It only means our descriptions and explanations of that world derive from fallible human minds; thus, all knowledge is subjective.

In his book *The Philosophy of Physical Science*, astrophysicist Arthur Eddington noted that the knowledge physical scientists create is subjective. At the same time, he explained that scientists seek to discover absolutes, albeit subjective absolutes.[2]

The existence of absolutes does not imply objective knowledge. Fallible people create absolutes. Many reasonable intellectuals claim scientific knowledge is objective. But how do they define *objective*? Is it knowledge about which everyone agrees? Is it knowledge that's been tested and confirmed countless times? Or would it be a repository of perfect knowledge that exists in a mysterious realm beyond the reach of mere mortals?

The problem with all versions of objectivity is that no scientific explanation, even those that seem rock solid, is ever the final word. Every current best explanation—those most widely accepted by educated people—is subject to evolutionary improvement and replacement. As British mathematician George Box once said, "All models are wrong, but some are useful."

We cannot disprove the existence of a repository of perfect Platonic knowledge that may exist somewhere in the universe and into which our minds may reach in some way we cannot characterize and have never observed. But such speculations are beyond the bounds of scientific discourse. They are metaphysical religious concepts. Science does not deal with such unverifiable speculations.

Gottfried Wilhelm Leibniz, Andrew Galambos, and David Deutsch developed logical proofs that acquirable knowledge is infinite, which means, in the words of Deutsch, we are always near the beginning of infinity. Objective or perfect knowledge divorced from the limitations of the human mind is a philosophical version of heaven or nirvana, a mythical place in which all our desires are satisfied. From my point of view, that is a perfect description of hell. If all our desires were satiated, we would have nothing to do. Intelligent beings need challenges. Our purpose is to figure out how to deal with them such that we can survive and continue creating and building.

The survival of civilization depends on developing a science of social systems, a domain arising from individuals pursuing goals derived from their vision of happiness. If it's going to be a science, it must be built upon absolutes and universals, few though they may be. Let's first establish precise definitions of *good*, *bad*, and *value* in the context of absolute morality.

Good: Any subjective preference of a person. It is whatever a person prefers over his current condition. It is his evaluation that, given anticipated costs, he would prefer to exchange his current condition for one he thinks will be better. What people consider good is relative to their frame of reference. There is no such thing as a universal good.

Bad: The opposite of good. It is anything people prefer to avoid. It is their evaluation that the potential transition to a given condition would be worse than their current condition.

Value: Preferences that are relative to each person. One person's values may have little or even negative value to someone else. There are no absolute or eternal values.

When studying human behavior, we notice each person has distinctive preferences that differ from everyone else's. What each person calls *good* is relative to his frame of reference. Each person pursues his idiosyncratic vision of happiness. The specifics of everyone's preferences constantly change as they adapt to new information and adjust their actions accordingly.

Among the many valid explanations of volitional phenomena are the principles underlying property exchanges. It seems common sense that exchange results from two people who place the same value on the goods being traded. Yet, if we look a little deeper, we find economic exchange only occurs when the parties differ over the *relative* value of the objects being exchanged. When customer A buys toothpaste from store owner B, it means A values the toothpaste more than the money it costs. The reverse is true for B. He values the money more than the toothpaste.

Per Carl Menger, each person has unlimited preferences or goods he mentally arranges in an implicit ordinal list and rearranges as he receives new information. The first item on the list is whatever he feels is most urgent to pursue at the moment and is revealed through his actions.

Preferences and Prices

Our desires are never satiated. We exist in a permanent state of dissatisfaction. Once we get what we believe will make us happy, new desires arise. Dissatisfaction is what motivates us to act. It's what motivates us to build, create, and innovate. It's also what motivates some people to steal, deceive, and murder.

The list of values or preferences is a mental tool that helps us explain what happens when we act. The key concept is ordinal, which means to arrange in a certain order, i.e., first, second, third. It would be absurd to attempt to quantify or measure the intensity or size of our preferences with mathematical precision. There are no absolute cardinal (quantitative) units of value, goodness, desire, or utility. Without such units, we can't measure the objective value of our preferences and compare them to someone else's. All we can do is infer that Bill prefers X over everything else at that moment since he's pursuing X. Sally prefers Y over everything else since she is pursuing Y.

One of the fascinating aspects of the social world is how prices, an all-embracing measurement system, arise naturally from everyone's subjective preferences. The global system of prices captures the results of every transaction and turns them into constantly updated, unambiguous numbers. It's an information system signaling the relative demand for and availability of every product, service, skill, or natural resource. Markets account for everyone's preferences and register the integrated results in changing prices everyone can use. Prices are measured by money, a unique product that emerged from individual transactions when people began using certain goods, e.g., gold, silver, cattle, and cowrie shells, as a medium of exchange.

Markets allow for the optimal satisfaction of many different desires by enabling widespread cooperation. They are the most effective way an intelligent species satisfies, to one degree or another, the enormous diversity of tastes and values. We register a preference when we choose to buy or not buy any product or service. We are not imposing our choice on anyone else. (Compare that to political voting, in which a majority imposes its preferences on everyone else.)

Social and economic theorists have tried to develop a quantitative unit of value or utility for centuries. They sought to measure objective value to create a social system they could mathematically analyze to figure out how to deliver the greatest good to the most people. But no one has ever devised a useful operational definition of such a unit because it can't be done.

Consider how you choose to go to one movie instead of another. Your feelings signal you'd prefer to watch movie A. If you sense your partner would rather watch movie B, you may choose to please that person rather than insist on your preference. Thus, intersubjective (between different people) comparisons of value, goodness, or happiness are not possible or even desirable. The key point is that everyone determines for their own reasons what actions they believe will lead to greater satisfaction. No one else can choose what's good for another person. Of course, one can delegate such authority in more complex or difficult conditions, as one might do with a surgeon or investment manager.

In volitional science, a person's values are an ultimate given. They are the basis of action. A major purpose of any social system is to enable everyone's differential pursuit of happiness while minimizing conflict. That raises a critical question: How do we resolve the inevitable conflicts arising from billions of people each pursuing his own unique vision of happiness? For a theory of the social domain to be valid, it must provide a universal basis for conflict resolution.

Conflict Resolution

How can we resolve conflict? The question leads to a common justification for state coercion. Supporters of a state, such as Thomas Hobbes, claim that to preserve social harmony, we need an institution with a monopoly on violence and the supreme authority to resolve disputes.[3]

But is it possible to resolve disputes and conflicts without resorting to violence or the threat of violence? The answer derives from one of Galambos's greatest achievements: a secular standard of absolute morality. You'll recall that in volitional science, we define *absolute morality* as the minimal set of rules governing behavior that, when instantiated across an entire society, is necessary and sufficient for it to evolve into a civilization that can survive and prosper indefinitely. Methods derived from those rules will allow people to resolve conflicts in the absence of a supreme coercive authority, such as a state.

Even in today's partially free markets, most people transact business in a nonviolent, non-fraudulent way because they find it more profitable. By more profitable, we mean the action results in greater happiness for all parties involved. Some claim that people behave morally due to religious or philosophical beliefs. That may be true; however, if their ethical norms left them poorer and less satisfied, the behavioral effect of such beliefs would quickly fade.[4]

All actions entail consequences, which can be good or bad from each person's point of view. As the ramifications of billions of actions accumulate, they will affect the cohesion and effectiveness of the social order. Here are examples of consequences we can predict in probabilistic terms:

- When word gets out that an accountant creates fraudulent financial statements, most people will choose to avoid dealing with him, resulting in his loss of reputation and wealth.
- The more a political state taxes production, the less production there will be. Entrepreneurs will have less capital to reinvest in their businesses and less incentive to work harder to serve their customers.
- The more a state coercively regulates businesses, the more entrepreneurs will be demotivated. Production will tend to decline, resulting in decreased prosperity and increased poverty.
- In a free market, prices are a function of supply and demand. If the price of a good goes up, all other things being equal, the demand for the good will go down. If the price of a good falls, the demand for the good will rise.
- Every political law or coercive policy instituted to achieve X will, over time, achieve the opposite of X because political laws and regulations interfere with

the interconnected networks of people pursuing happiness. A coercive law does one of two things. It either (a) forbids people from doing something they want to do or (b) forces people to do something they would prefer not to do. In simple terms, that's why coercive laws and regulations produce results that are opposite to those intended.

It may come as a shock to political activists and social engineers to learn the social world is governed by natural laws just as ironclad as those of the physical and biological worlds. When you violate them, you will not get the results intended. If you dream up a socialist utopia in blissful ignorance of the natural laws of the social domain, it will end in acrimony and collapse, often accompanied by bloodshed. Capitalism begins with the premise of every man for himself and ends up with harmonious global cooperation. Socialism begins with the premise of harmonious cooperation and ends in the chaos of every man for himself.

Political systems increase coercion over time in a futile attempt to rectify the failure of previous policies. The failure of coercion breeds more coercion, which breeds more failure.[5] There are two categories of coercive action: Force is interfering with an owner's control of his property, including his life, by using or threatening to use physical violence. Fraud is the use of deception to interfere with an owner's control over his property. In volitional science, an immoral act is any act involving coercion. Therefore, any volitional act that is not immoral, i.e., noncoercive, is a moral act. A moral act entails no interference with the property of an owner. Moral acts give rise to a civilization of freedom.

Property Rights

Right: The principle that the person who creates specific, identifiable property (the owner) controls its use to the exclusion of everyone else until the owner transfers the right to someone else.

The concept of a right is derived from absolute morality. Each person has a right to control his property to the exclusion of everyone else. In essence, that means there's a right not to be coerced. No one else may interfere with the right of exclusion and control. This is not a legal concept to be enforced by the state. Its exclusionary zone is not enforceable by legal coercion. Rather, it is a customary principle people will honor because they find complying with it more profitable. The consequences of violating this right will not be coercive but will result in a form of justice far more severe, swift, and productive than state "justice," also known as "injustice." That is already true in today's markets. When someone has a reputation for fraud and dishonesty, productive people avoid dealing with him. In a civilization of freedom, criminals will be shut out of the benefits of progress without resorting to police, courts, prisons, or execution.

When people feel secure in their property, they are more willing to offer it in the market. Otherwise, they will not enjoy the profit and self-esteem derived from providing value to others. Property rights have a proven track record of success over thousands of years. For example, British common law underpinned a culture of prosperity that, by the end of the nineteenth century, had given rise to the most fruitful scientific culture and the highest standard of living the world had ever seen.

Property rights derive from natural creative effort rather than arbitrary legal conventions. They disperse responsibility across the entire population. They also accord with justice. Who has a greater claim to control any property than its creator? Property rights embody justice because the person who creates or produces a thing controls the terms under which others can use it. Someone is going to control the usage of every bit of property people create. Who better to have that authority than the one who created or produced it? Major property creators will hire contractual agents to help manage their property estates. Most creators will want to maximize their long-term financial return by generating ongoing and growing value for consumers.

Property rights and the principle of ownership provide an absolute standard of morality. They draw a distinct, easily interpreted boundary separating moral and immoral actions. Either a person's actions interfere with the property of another, in which case they are immoral, or they do not, in which case they are moral.

Absolute morality entails only one rule governing behavior: respect property. Do not interfere with someone else's property, ever. Historically speaking, the stronger and more pervasive property rights are, the more a society exhibits peace, prosperity, artistic creativity, and scientific innovation. The converse is also true. Higher levels of coercion and weaker property rights have always resulted in poverty, violence, and war.

For an absolute standard of morality to be pragmatic, people must be able to apply it in all their interactions. Property rights are noncontradictory in that when property boundaries are clear, one person's right to control his property does not conflict with another person's similar right. The problem, until now, is there's never been a simple, precise explanation connecting morality with property ownership. No one has identified a universal principle everyone could use to govern interactions. Without a well-defined understanding of the connection between property rights and morality, state and religious coercion has always eroded property ownership until a society collapsed.

The Golden Rule

The concept of absolute morality is a reformulation of the Golden Rule into a simple, precise principle via the mechanisms of property and ownership. It is one of Galambos's key innovations. His is a secular idea, independent of theological, mythological, or mystical beliefs. Nevertheless, it does correspond to the Golden Rule—the rule of reciprocity—a concept that appeared long before Jesus of Nazareth. For example, in the sixth century BCE, Thales of Miletus, whom most historians of science consider the world's first scientist, claimed the supreme principle of morality was to "avoid doing what you would blame others for doing."[6]

The Golden Rule, in one form or another, has been a foundational principle of every historically significant culture. It is based on the reciprocal nature of human interaction. There are two versions of the Golden Rule. The version attributed to Jesus can be misapplied in obnoxious, immoral ways: "In all things, do unto others as you would have them do unto you." The problem is that I may not like what you like and might prefer that you would not do it to me. This formulation can encourage busybodies, known today as "Karens," to impose their values on others.

The second, better version is more common and favored by secular philosophers. Thales in sixth-century BCE Greece, Lao Tzu and Confucius in fifth-century BCE China, the Judaic philosopher Hillel in the first century CE, and Thomas Hobbes in the sixteenth century all espoused the double negative version, which states: "Do **not** do unto others what you would **not** want them to do to you."[7]

As eloquent and wise as this sentiment is, it is far from a scientific principle. For one thing, it is not precise and thus subject to multiple interpretations. The coercive way it has been used violates the principle itself. For another, it has not worked. Has Chinese society been characterized by an absence of strife, tyranny, war, slavery, or crime at any time? Has the behavior of Christians been directed into bloodless channels? World War I, a conflict in which both sides were Christian, resulted in the slaughter of more than thirty million people.

Absolute morality is a logically rigorous reformulation of the double negative version of the Golden Rule. It is also equivalent to the liberal notion of laissez-faire, which roughly translated means leave people alone or, more bluntly, butt out of my life unless I invite you in.

Absolute morality is pragmatically consistent. By this, I mean that when applied in the real world, exercising any one right in the set of rights does not conflict with someone else's exercise of the same or another right. Contrast that with rights granted by political authority. For example, a right to health care would enslave doctors who would no longer be free to practice their profession in ways they considered best for their patients. A right to free speech could be curtailed by political rulers who proclaim an overriding right to be protected against misinformation or hate speech—and they determine what constitutes either or both.

The concept of absolute morality in volitional theory allows for an infinite number of potential courses of action. It is a constraint, but one that opens up myriad possibilities by protecting creativity and high production from the threat of violence and fraud. It is a moral standard that applies to every intelligent species that may exist anywhere in the universe.[8] As such, it is a **universal standard of morality**. No species can expand into the cosmos until it has implemented absolute morality across its entire society as the customary governing principle of interactions.

Ownership and Progress

By asserting the principle that an owner's control of his property is inviolate, absolute morality fosters a social system of scientific innovation and creativity. Property boundaries give rise to proprietary incentives, enabling us to resolve all societal and environmental problems without violence. Of course, given that progress in a civilization of freedom is open-ended and of boundless possibility, today's solutions will always generate new challenges to pursue and new problems to solve. Ignorance always expands faster than the growth of knowledge.

The frontier beyond which we know little or nothing will always be greater than it was before. Isaac Newton, who produced the greatest expansion of useful knowledge in human history, articulated that principle in a personal and very moving way: "I do not know what I may appear to the world; but to myself I seem to have been only like a boy playing on the sea-shore, and diverting myself in now and then finding a smoother pebble or a prettier shell than ordinary, whilst the great ocean of truth lay all undiscovered before me."[9]

For the most significant class of property, ownership is perpetual and cannot be transferred. Ownership of ideas and their specific embodiments in such things as technical inventions or works of art cannot be traded or given away. For example, scientific theories, inventions, novels, paintings, movies, and musical compositions are the property of their creator in perpetuity. Isaac Newton will forever own his laws of motion, the law of gravitation, the calculus, which he shares with Leibniz, and his many other major insights. Those ideas are his property.

In volitional science, ownership results from a person's creation of something new, and that ownership is perpetual. Neither the creator nor his estate can trade his ownership away. Mark Twain is the author and, thus, owner of *Huckleberry*

Finn, The Mysterious Stranger, and many other works. It would be absurd to assert that Twain could transfer the authorship of his work to someone else. Authorship is historical fact, and authorship means ownership.

However, the *use* of ideas may be licensed in exchange for a royalty. The type and size of such royalties would be determined by an innovator's customers, who will be entrepreneurs for the most part. As I explain in chapter 9, those customers will choose the amount and type of royalties they will pay in the long run. To be sure, the authors of ideas, scientific theories, inventions, and artistic works can publish and sell copies of their work for any price they want. Such transactions do not transfer ownership of the intangible semantic or artistic content of their innovations.

Standards of Morality

All prior standards of morality have been relative standards that restricted human action to a small set of known behaviors approved by the religious or political authorities of a given era. That's why most prior societies have stagnated, trapped in endless cycles of impoverishment. Such relative standards boiled down to the ruling authorities' ideological or religious whims, backed by force.

A clear sign a standard of morality is relative and not absolute is that it is imposed on people by force, fraud, or both. Absolute morality cannot be imposed on anyone because doing so would be immoral, thus self-contradictory. Religious standards of morality are often promulgated by men who claim to have received God's word, which, out of the goodness of their hearts, they will share with the rest of us. These authorities claim God demands we obey them and adhere to their restrictive rules of behavior or else. The "or else" implies we will be condemned to torture, imprisonment, seizure of our property, or martyrdom. Or, as in the case of Giordano Bruno, all the above. In today's world, those who violate the ever-changing standards of political correctness may be drummed out of their professions, lose their social media accounts, and even be charged with high crimes and misdemeanors. They are prevented from earning a livelihood.

With theological and political ideas of morality, disagreement between different tribes or countries is the rule rather than the exception. Such disagreements are usually resolved by the threat of violence or actual bloodshed. Both sides to the dispute often claim they are following the command of an omniscient, omnipotent deity or an unobservable, undefined abstraction called the nation, the *volk*, Marx's "material productive forces," or Rousseau's "general will" (*la volonté générale*).[10] If you don't follow the leader's orders, the authorities claim you are violating God's will or betraying your social class. Thus, you will be accused of treason and jailed or executed.

Legality and traditional ethics are not the same as morality. Customary ethics are the pragmatic heuristics people develop to apply a moral standard to specific domains of human behavior. Traditional ethics are often congruent with absolute morality, but political legality rarely is. With political laws, what is legal is frequently immoral, and what is moral is frequently illegal. For example, in almost all societies, killing a human being is illegal, which accords with absolute morality. However, state law enforcement agents can kill without recourse due to the legal concept of sovereign immunity. And soldiers may kill with impunity anyone the state deems an enemy. We get repeated mass murders called war, which are legal but immoral.

Only states start wars; profit-seeking companies do not. If a private company were to start a war, it means it has given up the pursuit of profit and turned to plunder and the pursuit of coercive political power. The company has become a state or a crime syndicate, but I repeat myself. All over the planet, state agents regularly confiscate a large portion of their fellow citizens' wealth. This massive theft, called taxation, is legal but immoral. In a civilization of freedom, solutions will never involve coercion. No one will kill or confiscate property to protect it.

★ ★ ★

Recap

- Absolute morality is the minimal set of rules governing individual behavior that a volitional species must adopt for its civilization to survive and prosper indefinitely.
- *Absolute* does not imply the final word on any subject. Science is an open-ended market of people freely innovating and organizing ever-better explanations of natural phenomena. Still, the pursuit of physical, biological, and volitional absolutes assumes an orderly universe governed by laws we can discover and apply to useful ends.

- According to volitional science, the survival of civilization depends on developing social systems wherein individuals are free to pursue what they believe will increase their happiness as long as they do not interfere with an owner's property. People make choices that derive from their subjective evaluation of whether something is good or bad.
  - Value: Preferences that are relative to each person
  - Good: Anything an individual prefers or desires
  - Bad: The opposite of good, anything an individual seeks to avoid
- Prices are a natural way to measure preferences. They capture the results of every transaction people undertake and turn them into constantly updated numbers. It's a powerful information system signaling the relative demand for and availability of every product, service, skill, or resource people may want to use.
- Volitional science holds that a major purpose of social systems is to facilitate everyone's ability to pursue their own version of happiness while providing a universal basis for conflict resolution.
- Absolute morality has one rule governing behavior: respect property. Do not interfere with someone else's property, ever. That is the Golden Rule expressed via the mechanisms of property and ownership. That is a minimal set of general rules: one.
- The concept of a right as derived from absolute morality means the presumption that each individual may control his own body and all property he creates to the

exclusion of everyone else. That implies a right not to be coerced. We may protect that right with noncoercive market means alone.

- Absolute morality fosters a social system of scientific innovation and creativity. When people are secure in their ownership of what they produce, they will create more things of higher quality. Secure property boundaries can resolve all societal and environmental problems without violence.

- A clear sign that a standard of morality is relative and not absolute is that it's imposed by force, fraud, or both. Absolute morality cannot be imposed on anyone because doing so would be immoral.

4

Two Postulates of Volitional Science

We speak not strictly and philosophically when we talk of the combat of passion and of reason. Reason is, and ought only to be the slave of the passions, and can never pretend to any other office than to serve and obey them.

—David Hume

ANDREW GALAMBOS DETERMINED that a useful science of volition can be derived from two fundamental postulates. Before I state those postulates, I must lay some groundwork.

Subjective Knowledge and Social Cooperation

It's important to understand that volitional science is a logical science akin to Euclidean geometry. As with geometry, its conclusions and derivative theorems must fit observable reality and explain it better than other explanations. The challenge is to capture the fundamental element of subjectivity and intention at the base of human action in simple assertions from which everything else can be derived.

Subjective may seem outside the purview of science. Most scientists assume scientific knowledge must be objective. Let's revisit that assumption. Someone created every bit of knowledge we possess today by processing inputs from the outside world through their mind. The explanations that constitute our knowledge, the most valuable tool we use to survive and prosper, are subjective at the most fundamental level.

Subjective has almost become a verboten word in scientific circles. Certain people recoil at the mention of it. Yet, to understand the world of volitional beings and the social systems they create, there's no avoiding the subjective nature of human action. Since the pursuit of knowledge is a volitional endeavor, it, too, is inescapably subjective. Scientific knowledge is subjective, including the laws we consider universal. We can only come up with better explanations; we can never produce the final ultimate truth. We will never discover the notorious "theory of everything." We will always have to deal with receding frontiers of ignorance, which is a blessing, not a curse. To learn and explain more about our world until the end of time is our supreme purpose. Even "the end of time" is a chimera. As we learn more, who knows? Perhaps we will learn enough to keep pushing back forever, forever.

When someone conceives what they believe to be a better explanation of a certain natural phenomenon, they submit it to peers for criticism, testing, further development, and technical applications. While every new idea or explanation originates in one person's mind, the ultimate result emerges from written and verbal exchanges. Such exchanges might range from discussions about weaknesses in the new explanation to formulating various tests of the hypothesis and analyzing the results. Scientific theories emerge and evolve from a market dynamic.

That said, we must not lose sight of the fact that all innovation originates in the minds of specific people. The concept of subjectivity says we are constrained in what we can know about the world by the limits of our sensory equipment. We can only assess that data through the inherent mental abilities of a mind that emanates from our physical neurology, which was shaped by biological evolution and, to a smaller, later extent, by cultural evolution. Both systems—our sensory receptors and mental apparatus—have resulted from several billion years of ruthless competition to survive and reproduce in a world of relative scarcity.

The most limiting scarcity has never been natural resources, including our access to energy. These are abundant. As long as we maintain enough freedom to think and innovate, we will never run out of energy or material resources, which, as Einstein showed, are interchangeable. Our greatest scarcity has always been our meager knowledge of the world. Throughout history, a few minds driven by the desire to survive have produced better explanations that have reduced ignorance and produced more effective ways to survive and thrive.

Evolution has molded minds that work well enough to have produced the astonishing fruits of scientific, technological, and economic progress we enjoy today. Our cognitive faculties can create knowledge that reflects aspects of our world relevant to our survival and prosperity. Even better, when our explanations are subject to market acceptance, including peer testing and criticism, they become even more valuable over time. For example, Newton's explanations of the physical world are embodied in an ever-greater number of products and services every year. SpaceX engineers its rockets and satellites using Newtonian science for the most part.

Markets represent social collaboration. They are natural systems rising from people interacting with each other to produce and trade goods and services in pursuit of greater satisfaction. When we examine these transactions, we can see that all nonviolent trade is based on the custom of ownership, whether implicit or explicit. If you don't own, and thus control, the goods or services you're offering, how can you exchange them?

We now know human social systems are constrained and shaped by universal natural laws of social cooperation. A refusal to accept the existence of such constraints, such as absolute morality (respecting an owner's control over his property), is one reason every prior political system has failed. Humans thought they could apply just the right amount of coercion to construct society however they wished. If the rulers—be they a congress, a parliament, or a dictator—decreed something, that would bring it into being. However, when people disregard the natural constraints of the laws of nature by accepting state coercion as a viable means of achieving their ends, they will not get the results intended.

The natural laws of social cooperation are as immutable as those of the physical and biological domains. If we act as if they don't exist, we will meet with disaster. The failure will be all the more catastrophic if we resort to coercion because, in doing so, we undermine the most important survival tool ever discovered: open-ended markets of human cooperation.

Given the essential role of the individual, we must start with an analysis of individual behavior to develop a useful explanation of social systems. Volitional science does this by asserting two postulates that explain human behavior at the most fundamental level.

The first postulate of volitional science is a universal description of human action and what motivates that action. Saying it is *universal* means it applies to every possible action every volitional being could take everywhere in the universe.

A **postulate** is an assumption asserting a universal self-evident truth. For the assumption to be valuable, every one of its logical derivatives must lead to useful explanations. If we can find one exception, our assumption is defective and must be modified or scrapped. The assumption must be simple and clear. A complex postulate could be true, but with every new layer of complexity, we narrow the range of applicability and make it more difficult to use. Every important theory, explanation, or application in the social world derives from the two postulates of volitional science.

FIRST POSTULATE

First Postulate: Volitional beings act to pursue greater happiness.

Volition is making choices based on the expectation of gain or avoidance of loss. What constitutes a gain or loss is relative to each person. By its nature, volition is a characteristic of individuals alone. It is a subjective, often subconscious, evaluation people use to choose their course of action. Even when acting in a collaborative enterprise such as a business, the larger structure is an abstraction reflecting the result of people choosing to cooperate for idiosyncratic reasons. An abstract entity does not choose anything. Only individuals at various levels and positions in the enterprise evaluate, choose, and act.

The first postulate of volitional science is a simple, universal description of the nature of volitional action. Every action you will ever undertake is in pursuit of greater happiness. You are doing that all the time, and you can't help it. Society emerges from people pursuing happiness. We can define a successful social system as one that enhances its members' ability to pursue their version of happiness without conflicting with others' ability to do the same.

Happiness is the integrated totality of a person's preferences at any time. What one person calls good, another person may consider bad. Happiness is a volitional being's subjective evaluation of all experiences in memory and all anticipated "goods" and "bads" diluted by time and proprietary importance. While we each have a general view of happiness that persists over time, it evolves as we develop new interests, learn new things, or face unforeseen challenges. We each have a constantly updated happiness balance sheet.

Satisfaction is the term we use to describe a person's state of happiness at any moment. When we act, we are always—100 percent of the time—pursuing greater satisfaction. The first postulate asserts this to be a universal characteristic of human action and uses it as the basis of the logical system of volitional science.

Happiness can never be fully attained. A being who is completely happy or satisfied would not act. All action stems from dissatisfaction, large or small, with our present condition, coupled with the ability to imagine a more satisfactory situation and the belief that there are available means to achieve it. Every conscious action, from changing our position in a chair to changing careers, is taken in pursuit of greater happiness.

Let's deal with some common objections to the claim of universality for the first postulate. The most obvious is suicide. But this is not a failure of the postulate. Someone who kills himself sees nothing but pain and misery ahead and prefers death as the only way to avoid that fate. A major part of pursuing happiness is avoiding emotional and physical pain. Some may also commit suicide as an act of perverse revenge. Others may believe blowing themselves up in a crowd of infidels will send them to paradise. One could think of many variations on these themes, but in each one, the actor seeks what he believes will be a better state than the one he's in.

Another possible objection to the first postulate applies to someone who chooses an ascetic life of self-denial. But she, too, is pursuing her version of happiness. She's seeking what she sees as the higher things in life. She believes that pursuing bourgeois material desires would interfere with her higher calling. When someone lives an ascetic life of self-denial, it accords with the first postulate.

A third objection comes from more educated circles. Some will insist the first postulate is a tautology. We can only observe a person's actions; we cannot observe what motivated those actions. So, we interpret whatever end he's pursuing as something he considers more satisfactory. We know what he prefers only by observing his actions, from which we deduce whatever he's pursuing is the thing or condition he thinks will bring him greater happiness. It seems as if we're going around in circles. Are we?

In any logical system, such as Euclidean geometry, once we settle on the postulates, every logically deduced derivative is already inherent in the postulates. Yet, no one would deny that Euclidean geometry is one of the most valuable creations of the human mind. The engineers who designed and built the Golden Gate Bridge in the 1930s used geometry at every phase of the construction. Every building, bridge, or other material artifact of human ingenuity was created using Euclid's geometry. Being tautological did not detract from its value in the slightest.

The pertinent aspect of the first postulate is its identification of happiness as subjective. Each person's vision of happiness is unique. Every intentional action is someone's pursuit of greater happiness. The explanations we derive from this postulate are the richest and most powerful explanations of the social world ever conceived, especially when combined with the second and more important postulate.

Individuals and Individual Action

Any useful, scientific explanation of the social domain must begin with an analysis of the individual and individual actions. One of the major reasons the social sciences have not delivered on their promise is their failure to recognize this. In focusing on the individual, I'm not referring to *homo economicus* or the "economic man" caricature developed by neoclassical economists. Volitional science focuses on real, fallible humans with an endless variety of values, preferences, skills, weaknesses, and personalities from which we derive the universal quality captured by the first postulate: the pursuit of subjective happiness.

We begin our analysis of the social realm with the individual because only individuals act, evaluate, and choose. People and their actions are observable. Everyone has a discrete, identifiable physical body. Social collectives are real things that influence action but aren't concrete, observable entities. They are abstractions that do not think, prefer, choose, or act. Collectives do not choose to pursue anything. Collectives are not volitional. Social collectives are a result of individuals pursuing happiness.

This brings up a major difference between the biological and social domains. When cells join to form an organism, it's a result of physical and chemical processes. Once joined, cells exist as subsidiary components of an animal's or plant's body. A cell can't decide to leave a body to live in someone else's body or to enjoy life as a single-celled organism. Cells have no autonomous mind.

It is different when volitional beings join or identify with a larger social collective, whether a profit-seeking company, a political movement, or a religion. People may join or identify with a religion, nation, ethnic group, professional class, or many other collectives. They can also decide to leave or cease identifying with such groups, even if threatened with violence or death. The authorities cannot make a free-thinking person think like an acolyte. Collectives emerge from personal decisions. Their influence expands or shrinks for the same reason.

Of course, our choices are constrained by cultural and political factors. They also depend on our innate abilities, level of intelligence, etc. The physical and biological domains also limit our options. But volitional beings know they have options even when all their choices seem bad. In today's world, the most ubiquitous and harmful constraints derive from coercion, particularly institutional coercion. When political authorities threaten to kill or imprison people if they leave the tribe or refuse to pay the tribute demanded, they enslave those people. They are treating them as nonthinking cells in a larger social body or as mechanical components in a giant social machine. They are not treating people as volitional beings with values and aspirations.

A social system can support or obstruct a person's pursuit of greater satisfaction. But it is absurd to talk about social collectives, such as nations, political states, or social classes, as having an existence independent of the individuals from which they arise.

I'm stressing this point because so much of today's social and political "science" analyzes the social world as if collectives think and act like individuals. It's a regressive relapse into mythical explanations. Such thinking leads to the assumption that people must subordinate their selfish desires to the more enlightened desires and values of the collective. But collectives have no desires or values. The truth is more banal. The beliefs of a collective are the beliefs of its leaders.

Such thinking derives from a mechanistic top-down approach to society, which I call *mechanical collectivism* to distinguish it from the bottom-up approach of *methodological individualism*. Using the latter, we have discovered the natural laws governing how social systems work. All such laws derive from an analysis that begins with a concept of individual volitional action and leads to social systems that maximize freedom. Individualism was the new idea from which classical liberalism arose during the Enlightenment. Volitional science makes possible a new twenty-first-century Enlightenment.

SECOND POSTULATE

Second Postulate: All pursuits of happiness that do not involve coercion are equally valid.

"The second postulate suggested itself to me from the theory of relativity," Galambos noted. "The theory of relativity in physics states something to this effect: all frames of reference are equally valid for formulating the laws of nature. That's exactly what the second postulate says applied to volition: all concepts of happiness that involve no immoral action are equally valid. Another way of saying that is all frames of reference that accord with morality are equally valid. The second postulate does not imply that all concepts of happiness are equally important or even reasonable."

This postulate asserts that all possible noncoercive, thus, moral actions a person may take are valid. It does not imply that any moral action is important, wise, urgent, or even coherent to anyone but the one pursuing it. Moral actions may even be self-destructive or damaging to an individual's longer-term happiness. It's moral for people to pursue all trivial forms of short-term happiness as long as they involve no coercion. Every action entails risk. People do things in all innocence that they later regret. These are called mistakes. We all make them and can learn from them, which is their deeper purpose.

The second postulate of volitional science can be called the morality postulate. Absolute morality must be the universal moral principle underlying any social system seeking to optimize cooperation, innovation, and freedom. These are the qualities necessary for a society to survive and prosper. No society has thus far successfully implemented rules of conduct derived from absolute morality. The ones that have come closest to this ideal, though, are always and everywhere more prosperous.

In the long run, there are only two alternatives for any life-form: grow or die. Stagnation and death result from social systems that suppress the ability to innovate and adapt. Refusing to evolve will result in the death of people and cultures. Until and unless an intelligent species adopts the noncoercion principle, it can never spread beyond its original birthplace in the cosmos. A social system with strong enough customary property rights will, at some point in its evolution, develop autocatalytic feedback systems that stabilize growth and lead toward greater freedom and cosmic expansion.

Absolute morality is latent in the structure of the universe. It is the universal rule of behavior that any volitional species must adopt on a customary basis if it is to avoid extinction and, per Elon Musk, become a spacefaring civilization. It's a natural law whose constraints are as absolute as the laws of physics. You can act in disregard of the laws of physics, but you will quickly meet with a bad end. You can also act in contradiction to the moral laws of social cooperation for a time, but you won't get the intended results and, sooner or later, will meet with catastrophe. You may delay the unintended consequences with ersatz fixes, but that will only result in worse societal calamities down the line as errors accumulate.

That's why continued violations of morality by politicians, bureaucrats, and generals become so disastrous in political systems. Coercion overwhelms, distorts, and destroys the natural feedback systems that support markets. People can violate the principle of noncoercion for a long time across broad swathes of society, projecting, for a while, an appearance of success. But the longer they do, the greater the ultimate negative consequences will be. The bigger they are, the harder they fall.

Political states are coercive parasites on productive people. Darwinian evolution regulates parasites to preserve the host's survival. The reason is simple: if the host dies, so do the parasites. Suppose a society has evolved a scientific and technical ethos upon which it depends for survival but retains a system of legal coercion. This means it has not developed a social order that protects property. Unless it develops a system to protect property, the parasitic coercion will spread and eat away at production until the host dies, as has happened throughout history.

Coercion does not work. It's morally abhorrent to most people and destructive to social order and production. If we aim to create a social system able to survive in a harsh, unforgiving universe, political coercion is the wrong tool.

Unpredictability

The second postulate allows for the open-ended, unpredictable nature of volitional life. It recognizes that everyone has a different vision of what actions will produce happiness for them. As long as those actions don't interfere with others, they are just as valid as anyone else's vision and the actions they pursue to achieve it.

We can never know the long-term ramifications of even the most trivial actions. Intelligence implies we are all ignorant and aware of our ignorance, even if we are afraid to admit it to ourselves or others. We live in a sea of uncertainty that we are constantly, often desperately, trying to make more certain.

An important derivative of our fundamental uncertainty is that trivial actions can have grave, unforeseen consequences or extraordinarily wonderful results. For a society to thrive, it must allow for the entire gamut of noncoercive actions. We cannot know the future entailments of even the most trivial actions.

In the mid-seventeenth century, German mathematician Gottfried Leibniz proved there are an infinite number of points between any two points on a line.[1] This implies there are an infinite number of such points in a person's life.

Because of the unidirectional nature of time, that's not true pragmatically, but it's close enough for the important concept I'm addressing. If you had made a different decision about a trivial matter at any point in life, it could have resulted in you marrying a different spouse, pursuing a different profession, or dying sooner than you otherwise would have. You can think of many times when a seemingly unimportant choice led to interactions with people and events that completely changed your life.

A powerful example of this aspect of reality turned out to have a positive, revolutionary effect on our history. During 1684, Edmond Halley, Christopher Wren, and Robert Hooke, in their pursuit of happiness, met in London from time to time to discuss a problem engaging the most brilliant thinkers of the era: What force would result in Kepler's elliptical planetary orbits? Halley and Hooke opined that the force must vary inversely with the square of the distance from each planet to the sun. Wren challenged them to produce a proof that the inverse square law led to elliptical orbits. Halley admitted he could not. Hooke claimed he'd conclusively proved it some years earlier. But when asked to produce his proof, he could not. Nor could he even outline his argument. Hooke said he thought Isaac Newton had worked on the problem for years but had not published any significant results. That led the ever-curious Halley to make a decision that changed the course of history.

Halley wrote to Newton, a notoriously reclusive professor of mathematics at Cambridge University, to ask if he could visit. Newton consented and received Halley at his quarters in Trinity

College. The younger man (Halley was twenty-eight and New-ton forty-two) put forward the question he, Wren, and Hooke had been debating and offered his view. Newton responded that Halley was correct and that he, Newton, had worked out a proof years earlier but was dissatisfied with it and had never arranged it for publication. He outlined his argument, which convinced Halley to the extent that he urged Newton to present an informal description of his proof to the Royal Society to establish his priority in such a momentous discovery.

Newton was reluctant. By then, he'd grown tired of defending his work against the nitpicking objections of little minds and had decided to publish no original work. But Halley's challenge stirred the sleeping lion into action. Over the next three years, Newton produced the most important book ever written, *Principia Mathematica*. Halley not only edited the book, which was not easy given Newton's demanding temperament, but he also financed and managed its publication.[2]

If Halley's curiosity had not led him to visit Newton, it's unlikely the *Principia* would have been written. It is the intellectual platform on which all subsequent scientific knowledge is based. Galambos called Newton and his publication of the *Principia* "the anchor point of history."

Innovation

We will never be able to predict what long-term effects may result from any action, even the most trivial. Galambos came up with the second postulate to reinforce the principle that for any intelligent species to thrive, it must develop a social system allowing individuals to pursue a maximal range of noncoercive pathways. By definition, innovation is a surprise. We can never know when it will happen or where it will lead. Hence, we should develop a social order that, at worst, does not inhibit innovators and, at best, supports them through noncoercive mechanisms.

On the other hand, we know coercive actions are destructive, even when they result in what appear to be positive outcomes. In the following illustration, I will use an example that Frédéric Bastiat used to illustrate his phrase "what is seen and what is not seen." If someone were to throw a rock through the window of a local bakery, it would make work for the glazier. That is what is seen. What is unseen but relevant is what the baker would have otherwise done with the funds he's now using to pay the glazier. He might have applied them to grow his business or take a long-needed vacation with his family. That is what is unseen.[3]

Now, apply that to the flawed social analysis economists use when they say things such as "World War II got us out of the Great Depression." Wrong! World War II caused untold destruction of lives and property and wasted untold amounts of capital on destructive weaponry. The more certain way to emerge from the Depression was to stop interfering in the economy and let the downturn run its course. As Ludwig von Mises explained, economic depressions are the cure for unbridled money creation, which leads to widespread misallocations of capital. Only when the deadwood is cleared out can economic growth begin again.

State coercion obstructs, and often prevents, experimentation and innovation, thus inhibiting progress in all branches of society. Once a political law is passed and a bureaucratic agency is set up to enforce it, innovation in that and adjacent sectors of the economy slows down and eventually ceases altogether. People will avoid risks if they're at risk of being imprisoned or fined for arbitrarily illegal entrepreneurial experiments. We will never know how many wonder drugs might have been developed over the past one hundred years if Harvey Washington Wiley and Theodore Roosevelt, with the best of intentions, had not created the precursor to the FDA. We will never know which novel therapies might have been developed in the absence of FDA bureaucrats. We might be enjoying longer, healthier lives today. In a freer society, medical innovators might have developed cures for heart disease, cancer, and neurological deterioration. That's the problem with state interventionism. We'll never know what might have happened in a civilization of greater freedom.

State bureaucrats force businesses into archaic, counterproductive methods of compensation. Federal and state laws mandate that corporations adopt a business structure that gives financial investors control over companies. In 2020, the California legislature passed a law making the use of independent contractors virtually illegal.[4] The purpose was to force workers to be employees paid an hourly wage with benefits dictated by the state. However, many people prefer the dignity of working as independent entrepreneurs who set their own hours. They may be happier working for less than what the government mandates because they may earn more in the long run if they work hard to satisfy customers.

There are myriad potential noncoercive pathways into the future. We can't know which will lead to important innovations, inventions, companies, products, and inspirational works of art. If we want civilization to survive and prosper, we must create a social system in which all moral actions are treated as valid. The corollary is that as coercion is gradually eliminated, each person will have to deal with the entailments, good or bad, of their choices. In freedom, no one will be forced to pay for another's decadent lifestyle. Individuals will have to pay the costs of whatever lifestyle they choose. This will improve a person's decision-making and lead to greater wisdom.

The second postulate is the basis of a social order that yields an endless variety of pursuits of happiness, no matter how trivial or important they may seem at the time. Morality does not limit humanity. Morality unleashes its potential for limitless creativity and expansion. If entrepreneurs can produce the high standard of living in today's first-world countries despite coercive bureaucracies taxing and constraining their actions at every turn, a far more advanced post-political form of capitalism will produce unimaginable wealth and consign poverty to the dustbin of history.

Civilization of Freedom

The first and second postulates are the basis of the science of volition. They are the foundation from which we can evolve beyond the current era of political barbarism into a peaceful, spacefaring civilization. Is such a civilization realistic? Am I being too idealistic? We already have millennia of experience with a less advanced version of such a social system. It's called the market. In various primitive forms, it has underpinned every successful culture throughout history. It will lead to new forms of government that compete for our business and adapt to evolving conditions.

Even if you like the idea of a free civilization devoid of coercion, you may think (1) it is too idealistic and (2) even if it would work as advertised, how could we attain such a civilization starting from our current system of massive political coercion? As to the first objection, if something qualifies as pragmatic if it works as predicted, then capitalism is pragmatic. People may complain all they want about predatory capitalism, but ask them from whom they buy their clothes, iPhones, etc. Most honest critics will admit markets deliver the goods!

Speaking of iPhones, Steve Jobs noted the value of business over politics: "None of the really bright people I knew in college went into politics. They all sensed that, in terms of making a change in the world, politics wasn't the place to be in the late Sixties and Seventies. All of them are in business now, which is funny because they were the same people who trekked off to India or who tried in one way or another to find some sort of truth about life."[5]

As for the second objection: How could we possibly achieve a civilization of freedom starting from a Flatland world of ubiquitous political coercion? It will be difficult but not impossible. It is contingent on attracting a few unusually competent visionary entrepreneurs who are seeking a challenge of this magnitude. It is they who will develop the profit-seeking companies that lay the foundations for a civilization capable of expanding into the cosmos. When these entrepreneurs understand that the alternative to the primary capitalism of Spaceland is almost certainly to be nuclear war or terminal economic collapse resulting in billions of deaths, they will shoulder the difficulties and enter history. We cannot survive without primary capitalism.

★ ★ ★

Recap

- Scientific knowledge is subjective, including the laws considered universal. All knowledge is created by people processing inputs from the outside world through their minds, meaning what we can know about the world is limited by our sensory and neurological equipment and thus subjective.
- First Postulate: Volitional beings act to pursue greater happiness.
  - Happiness is the integrated totality of a person's unique preferences at any time. Satisfaction is a person's current state of happiness. When we act, we are always pursuing greater satisfaction. All action stems from dissatisfaction with the present state and the pursuit of a more satisfactory situation.
  - Society emerges from people pursuing happiness. A successful social system enhances its members' ability to pursue their version of happiness without conflicting with others' ability to do the same.

o The individual pursuit of happiness is the proper basis for the social sciences, not social collectives, corporations, political parties, or religions. Individual action leads to social systems that maximize freedom, as seen in the individualism expressed in classical liberalism.

- Second Postulate: All pursuits of happiness that do not involve coercion are equally valid.

  o All possible noncoercive, moral actions people may take are valid. This doesn't mean every moral action is important, wise, or coherent to anyone but the person pursuing it. Any society that does not adopt the principle of noncoercion on a widespread basis will eventually collapse and disappear. For seven-to-ten thousand years of recorded history, every society or culture has been subject to political rule. All have disappeared.

  o The second postulate recognizes everyone has a different vision of what actions will produce happiness. As long as their actions don't interfere with others, they are just as valid as anyone else's vision and actions.

  o For society to flourish, all noncoercive actions must be allowed since we can't know the longer-term entailments of even the most trivial actions. They may have wonderful results or hideously negative consequences. This openness fosters innovation, the most effective tool for anyone who wants to survive and prosper in an expanding cosmic civilization. Coercion, on the other hand, is always restrictive and destructive. It prevents the experimentation and innovation that fuel progress. Political states are coercive parasites on productive people. Ask yourself: Where do they get all those trillions to spend on whatever they want?

- Volitional science offers the tools to better understand how social systems work and how those tools can be applied to create a civilization that survives and thrives. It posits that with a more advanced market system—primary capitalism—as the basis of civilization, humanity can grow and expand peacefully beyond Earth into the cosmos.

5

Entropy, Civilization, and Growth

Why the awe for the Second Law? The Second Law defines the ultimate purpose of life, mind, and human striving: to deploy energy and information to fight back the tide of entropy and carve out refuges of beneficial order.

—Steven Pinker

THIS CHAPTER DEALS WITH the larger context in which the science of volition analyzes social systems: the physical universe. The universe constrains and controls the biochemical nature of living organisms and what sort of social system(s) can support human flourishing in the long run. In volitional science, the *long run* means not just thousands of years but forever.

The first and second laws of thermodynamics are the most important physical laws affecting the behavior of intelligent beings and all living organisms. These laws were discovered during the nineteenth century by a series of innovative scientists, beginning with the great Sadi Carnot and his work on the efficiency of heat engines published in 1824.[1] Carnot's theoretical discoveries led James Joule, Hermann von Mayer, James Clerk Maxwell, Rudolf Clausius, William Thompson, Ludwig Boltzmann, and Josiah Willard Gibbs to develop the laws of thermodynamics as we know them today. Before their discoveries, social theorists did not have adequate knowledge to understand what would give rise to sustained growth in a lasting civilization of freedom and prosperity.

The physical universe is the larger context from which life and volitional beings get their purpose: to survive and prosper in a world that is often hostile to their well-being. That's what motivated our predecessors to develop a scientific understanding of the physical universe. The derivative innovations it produced allowed humanity to survive in far greater numbers than otherwise and produce a standard of living unimaginable to our ancestors.

If volitional beings are to create social systems that foster the widest possible cooperation over the long term, we must incorporate a proper scientific understanding of the physical, biological, and volitional universe into our theories. Since scientific knowledge results from an evolutionary process, we will never have a final explanation. However, during the five centuries since Copernicus published *De Revolutionibus* in 1543, scientific thinkers have come up with ever-better explanations of the universe as measured by the quantity and quality of products derived from those explanations. Imagine modern life without cars, airplanes, computers, mobile phones, and electrical distribution systems.

Entropy

In a later chapter, I will delve into the constraints the first law of thermodynamics imposes on social systems. Here, I will focus on the second law, which describes the fundamental directional flow of energy in the universe. Many of today's scientists believe, as Arthur Eddington explained, that the second law of thermodynamics holds "the supreme position among the laws of Nature."

> The law that entropy always increases—the second law of thermodynamics—holds, I think, the supreme position among the laws of Nature. If someone points out that your pet theory of the universe disagrees with Maxwell's equations, then it is so much worse for Maxwell's equations. If it is found to be contradicted by observation, well, these experimentalists sometimes bungle things. But if your theory is found to be against the second law of thermodynamics, I can give you no hope; there is nothing for it but to collapse in deepest humiliation.[2]

One of the fundamental discoveries of nineteenth-century science is how entropy (roughly, disorder) is a measure that allows us to quantify the directional flow of energy. That entropy always increases governs the fundamental flow of energy in the universe. The second law describes how energy flows "downhill" from concentrated orderly states to more dissipated randomized states. Energy flows governed by increasing entropy give birth to life and fuel its ongoing maintenance. Yet those same energy flows wear down and destroy life. They are the underlying cause of aging and death in complex biological organisms.

The flow of energy in the direction of dissipation also erodes the physical and social infrastructures of intelligent beings. The laws of the universe imply that unremitting effort is required on the part of living organisms to preserve their biochemical integrity and for volitional beings to maintain a resilient social system.

Life exists in the form of organisms, which are local units of complex, integrated energy systems imbued with a drive to survive by feeding off the natural energy flows described above. In the case of life on Earth, we access energy from our sun and stored heat energy rising from the Earth's core.[3] This survival instinct and the negentropic systems it engenders differentiate living systems from mere physical systems. Life creates lower entropy, more orderly systems in its local area, but as with everything in the universe, there's a cost. As life creates these protective islands of order, it accelerates the production of disorder in the rest of the universe. It does so to a greater degree than it decreases entropy in its local domain. On balance, life accelerates the production of entropy in the universe.

Intelligent beings accelerate this process even further by generating scientific knowledge and entrepreneurial markets to create and maintain the technical infrastructure needed for the sustained survival of billions of people. That requires a level of freedom that supports and protects such activities. Finally, they must develop ever-better ways to recycle the energy flowing through their civilization into reusable forms of matter and energy and exhaust the resulting waste into the vast, mostly empty universe.

Living organisms create and maintain local order at the expense of producing more heat energy than would otherwise exist. The ceaseless striving to access energy, apply it to maintain the growth of civilization, and deal with the waste resulting from that process constitutes the ultimate challenge for any intelligent species.

Boundaries

Boundaries have proven to be essential to prevent, or at least slow down, the breakdown and dissipation of order within individual organisms and the biosphere that supports their existence. That is also true for social systems and civilizations. The second law asserts that no energy transformation can be 100 percent efficient. There is always waste. If not disposed of properly, it will overwhelm and destroy order. Waste disposal and recycling will be one of the largest industries supporting our robust survival. In Spaceland, a myriad of profit-seeking companies will handle it.

All major civilizations have developed from social systems based on at least partially secure property boundaries. The utility of boundaries emerged billions of years ago in the first precursors of life when spontaneous chemical processes generated a flexible, selectively permeable lipid wall around a stabilized chain of chemical reactions. That series of stabilized reactions turned out to be the forerunner of the metabolic cycles powering all life on Earth. The lipid boundary evolved into the cell wall that protects the cyclical metabolic process that allows living organisms to survive, multiply, and evolve.[4] Cell walls protect the complex, orderly bio-chemical processes of life from natural entropic degradation and dissipation.[5]

Without that boundary and other forms of modularity, the evolution of complex life forms would not have been possible. Between six hundred million and a billion years ago, predation and the forces of natural selection began driving single-cell organisms to bind together into multicellular organisms.[6] Cells maintained their external boundaries as they combined into larger organisms. Modular construction resulted in flexible, adaptable living organisms that survived and reproduced at higher rates than other organisms by incorporating new levels of redundancy.

This change triggered an evolutionary explosion powered by natural selection in the direction of more complex organisms. According to Darwin, Wallace, and their successors, evolution toward greater complexity resulted from non-teleological random mutations and, once sexual reproduction evolved, phenotypes resulting from iterative genetic recombination with every new generation. In other words, it was not preordained that organisms would become more complex; the complexity came from the bottom-up process of Darwinian evolution, which enhanced the survival of those organisms that embodied it most effectively. Similarly, social systems develop from interactions without an overarching predetermined end state. All evolutionary systems, biological and cultural, must have (1) a way to generate novelty, (2) a method of selecting which new traits or innovations will survive, and

(3) the quality of being open-ended, meaning there is no predetermined end state.

We are here today because the boundary of the cell wall allowed cells to specialize and cooperate, albeit without conscious intention, in ever more complex organisms, each individual organism with its external boundary. That process culminated in human beings with volitional intelligence that evolved during the six million years after our hominid ancestors separated from the great apes.

Property boundaries are to societies of intelligent beings what the cell wall and other boundaries are to living systems. But there is an all-important difference. Cells are virtual slaves within an organism. Their cooperation is governed by the natural laws of the physical and biological domains. There's nothing voluntary about it. Volitional beings, on the other hand, can choose to cooperate or not. Yet, their choices are constrained by the laws of the volitional domain first articulated in modern times by the French physiocrats and thinkers of the Scottish Enlightenment, such as Adam Smith, David Hume, and Adam Ferguson. They were the first to discern that unless citizens learn to respect property boundaries, no social system can evolve into more sophisticated forms of creation and production.

Volitional science asserts that secure property boundaries are as important for social progress as cell walls are for the evolution of complex life. Secure property boundaries are a *sine qua non* for a volitional species to evolve a culture of prosperity and innovation. The key is recognizing that whoever creates X owns and controls the disposition of X.

Ownership identifies the individuals who control all the property within a specific boundary. Once owners feel secure in that control, they are incentivized to produce more and make their property available to others. Otherwise, they will see its value diminish over time. Hoarding never produces wealth for an owner. All forms of property increase in value the more people can access and apply them to productive purposes.

Cooperation

What does all this have to do with entropy? Living systems are engaged in an unceasing struggle to survive by protecting their bounded structural integrity against the wear and tear of entropic forces. Except for humans, organisms do this without conscious awareness in a competitive struggle to survive. Because individual organisms eventually lose the struggle and die, they evolved the ability to reproduce exact copies of themselves in the case of unicellular organisms and variable copies of themselves in the case of sexually reproducing multicellular organisms. Sexual reproduction accelerated evolution by providing natural selection with a greater variety of organisms from which to "choose."

Humans cooperate to build a vast array of interconnected protections against the forces of entropy. We create ever more efficient ways to access the energy flows that power our actions. We create knowledge that can be applied to make products, including a global technical infrastructure that allows Earth to support a current population of eight billion.

Perhaps the most important characteristic of volitional intelligence is that it facilitates cooperation. According to

Ricardo's law of association, intelligence lets us understand that cooperation is more advantageous than using force or fraud. Ricardo's Law states it's always more profitable for an advanced society to trade with a more primitive society rather than to plunder or enslave it. Slavery does not work if you want high production.[7]

The only realistic way to create the high level of cooperation necessary to counter the destructive force of entropy is through markets. Markets are cooperative social systems arising from harmonious, noncoercive property exchanges in pursuit of mutual profit. Financial profit is a natural measure of how effectively innovators and entrepreneurs are using available resources to serve others. Consumers' decisions to buy their products determine if they are creating value.

Without the recognition of property ownership, there's nothing to trade. In the absence of property rights that enable trade, whether of intangible intellectual property or tangible property, people revert to plunder, war, and alms (mooching) to get the means of existence. The problem with alms or donation mechanisms is their renunciation of profit. And ultimately, all alms (and taxes) come from the profits produced by entrepreneurs and innovators.

There has always been a mix of peaceful trade and plunder in every society thus far. Societies that exhibited a greater degree of peaceful trade and less coercion have enjoyed greater prosperity in material, commercial, scientific, and artistic terms. In contrast, those societies in which the state controlled and regulated commercial activity by force (a.k.a. socialism or fascism) have always been more impoverished.

Socialism: A social system in which the state controls all the means of production.

Fascism: A social system in which private individuals ostensibly own the means of production but are subject to the coercive control of state agents.

When property ownership is egregiously suppressed, as in the Soviet Union and other socialist or fascist countries, it spontaneously arises in everyday life. What's called the black market is the free market under tyranny. That's why both socialist and fascist societies require ubiquitous secret police forces to monitor citizens and suppress such activity. Yet, people working in small backyard plots, which the rulers were forced to allow to avoid famine, produced most of the food in the Soviet Union for much of the twentieth century.

Markets that emerge from secure property boundaries stimulate and support amicable cooperation between races, religions, and nationalities. They protect us from the forces of destruction and decay, such as war and theft. Voltaire's words in *Letters on England,* published in 1733, are apt.

Take a view of the Royal Exchange in London, a place more venerable than many courts of justice—where the representatives of all nations meet for the benefit of mankind. There the Jew, the Mahometan, and the Christian transact together, as though they all professed the same religion, and give the name of infidel to none but bankrupts. There the Presbyterian confides in the Anabaptist, and the Churchman depends on the Quaker's word. If one religion only were allowed in England, the Government would very possibly become arbitrary; if there were but two, the people would cut one another's throats; but as there are such a multitude, they all live happy and in peace.[8]

Capitalism

Capitalism is what we call the social system that develops from markets. In today's world, it has a pejorative meaning from the upside-down nature of education in our barbaric political world. Starting in elementary school, students are taught that capitalism is driven by greed to exploit the working class (whatever that is) and is evil. Thus, we need a political state to coercively regulate and control it. Yet, it is the only socioeconomic system that can support the evolution of civilization in a peaceful, autonomous manner.

Capitalism is on the side of negative entropy, orderliness, innovation, artistic creation, and production. Its incentives, based on property ownership and profit-seeking, motivate people to create, build, and expand the physical and societal order protecting us from the ceaseless forces of entropic destruction. In contrast, political systems escalate and intensify those destructive forces. States increase social disorder by supporting coercion and violence instead of peaceable cooperation.

Heretofore, we've had a primitive form of capitalism based on the partial ownership of tangible or secondary property. Although partial in that it allowed state interference, euphemistically called taxes and regulations, and did not acknowledge ownership of the most important form of property, intellectual property, this attenuated form of capitalism nevertheless facilitated widespread market cooperation across many political jurisdictions in Europe, Great Britain, North America, and eventually the entire world. That enabled the Western world (and now much of the developing world) to rise above the poverty and stagnation humans have endured for most of our history to create centuries of sustained progress.

It is now urgent that we initiate an entrepreneurial revolution if we are to survive and evolve beyond the existential crisis we face due to the almost universal belief in the necessity of institutional coercion. Entrepreneurs are the only class that can trigger such an evolution into a new form of capitalism that recognizes intellectual property ownership as the foundational basis of market cooperation. Historical and logical analyses show that once society recognizes that those who create property own it and control its distribution, market incentives will accelerate its transformation into goods and services that support peaceful survival and prosperity. Primary capitalism, based on the unrestricted ownership of intellectual property, can prevent scientific and technical knowledge from being applied in producing weapons of war and instruments of mass surveillance and oppression (see chapter 8). Furthermore, capitalist high production is the greatest defense against attacks from coercive societies. Freedom fosters technological innovation and prosperity, which are the most powerful deterrents against hostile societies ever conceived. Primary capitalism is the only realistic way to eliminate war, which we must do in a world awash with weapons of mass destruction.

When free from state interference, markets compensate people as a function of the value they produce for others. Scientific innovators have produced, by any measure, the most valuable property ever created. Yet, they have never been compensated in any way commensurate with the value they have delivered to the world. In a civilization capable of expanding into the cosmos, scientific and technical innovators will receive royalties from the applications of their ideas. They will end up with greater accumulations of capital than any other class of producer. To most political activists, that would be considered a bad outcome. Yet, who could better direct investment into funding research and innovative ventures aimed at breakthrough products than those with a track record of innovation? Of course, they will do so through competent assistants who are astute investors themselves, leaving the innovators free to continue innovating.

Primary capitalism is a new development but a natural progression from the partial capitalism we have enjoyed thus far. It is a natural evolutionary advance from the current system of "partial, secondary capitalism," which is collapsing under the weight of pervasive political interference in productive markets. Is it not suicidal that we appoint state bureaucrats and their enforcers to attack and harass the innovators and entrepreneurs who produce the only effective means of our survival?

Political states produce nothing except coercive interference in the productive activities of their citizens. State power produces a cultural devolution into a more primitive, violent existence. The problem with all political systems is their reliance on coercion to control and restrain behavior. The most productive and influential people today hold an erroneous belief in the necessity of political coercion. That gives bureaucrats license to overwhelm and eventually destroy the current system of partial capitalism that provides us with the products and services that sustain global prosperity.

Once an intelligent species develops physical science to the degree it can build weapons of mass destruction without having developed a social science of commensurate power that can explain how to prevent their use, it must choose between two possible futures. Either it will develop an effective science of social systems that allows it to evolve beyond political barbarism into advanced forms of primary capitalism, or it will not survive.

Since humans have applied physical science to develop such hideous devices as nuclear weapons, we can no longer tolerate a system of governance that accepts theft and war as valid tools of public policy. Although I doubt it, we may somehow muddle through and avoid nuclear war under our current dysfunctional political regimes. Yet, as long as there exists a pervasive belief in the efficacy of political states, even the most advanced societies will implode from the corrosive effects of institutional coercion.

Property and Profit

Primary capitalism is the key to survival because primary (intangible) property, particularly the cumulative knowledge expressed as scientific explanations, theories, and laws, is the most valuable property human beings have ever produced.

That's easy to see when we consider how engineers and entrepreneurs translate it into derivative technologies that improve our lives. The products derived from the scientific theories and explanations innovators create are the strongest confirmation of an idea's value. The act of consumers buying or not buying a product is the ultimate determinant of value. Why would anyone buy a company's wares unless the products enhanced their lives?

Primary property represents a far larger percentage of the value of all property than most would envisage. After all, the human imagination is the source of all other property. People create secondary (tangible) property by conceiving an idea or using someone else's ideas to produce new products. People create high-value primary property by building on the work of prior innovators, even when separated by thousands of years. Newton's invention of the calculus was built upon Archimedes' work on infinitesimals two millennia earlier.

Creating and disseminating primary (intellectual) property is the most important market in civilization and the societal basis of all progress. The market from which cumulative scientific knowledge arises is the basis of everything valuable in today's world. It stretches back to Thales of Miletus, Pythagoras, the unknown Hindu who invented the zero, Aristotle, Aristarchus, Euclid, Apollonius, Eratosthenes, and the greatest scientific mind of the ancient world, Archimedes.

The means to evolve into a peaceful spacefaring civilization must fit the ends. The process must be moral (noncoercive) and rely on the most effective means ever discovered to generate and maintain progress: a market of profit-seeking entrepreneurial ventures. Profit-seeking companies are effective because they align different skills and abilities into mutually profitable networks in pursuit of producing better goods and services that enhance our lives.

Like markets, profit is another natural tool built into the universe. It is a natural measure guiding organizations to utilize available resources to create products and services their customers will value. In a free capitalistic market, entrepreneurs either increase profits by serving people, a.k.a. customers, or they go out of business. Profit measures the value a company creates for others. The notion that high profits are obscene is absurd and destructive. If you earn extraordinarily large profits, it means you are serving people more effectively than other entrepreneurs.

No one knows what innovators and entrepreneurs will create, innovate, and develop in the future. Continual surprise within a stable societal context is the hallmark of open-ended capitalism. Virtually all future entrepreneurial ventures will derive from volitional theory. Freedom allows for an unlimited variety of profit-seeking businesses, including a countless array of noncoercive governments.

New profit-seeking corporations will be created that look nothing like today's legal corporations. They will derive from businesses far more advanced than the current dysfunctional, state-regulated corporations run by people with little or no skin in the game. The entrepreneurs and their associates who run future corporations will have skin in the game at every level of the enterprise.

These corporations will be regulated not by coercive bureaucrats but by the bonds of morality, profit, and imagination. Entrepreneurs will be free to experiment with new forms of compensation that incentivize rapid innovation. Associates working in a corporation will be connected by clearly written win-win/lose-lose contracts. Current win-lose employment with all its built-in conflicts will become as extinct as the dodo bird. These emergent new companies will result in higher degrees of freedom as bureaucrats gradually lose their power in the rising new entrepreneurial civilization.

Profit-seeking entrepreneurs possess an important but little-known strength in a coercive political world. States are completely dependent on them. They create all the wealth states confiscate to maintain their power. The reverse is not true. Profit-seeking companies don't need a state. Once they are free from the regulatory prison of state bureaucracies, they will produce at a far higher level. The best will generate gradually increasing profits for thousands of years.

Political States

We do not advocate fighting the state as a means of ending its barbaric ways. Fighting against what is wrong has never worked and never will. The exception to the rule is when dysfunctional political systems fail to anticipate and prevent an attack from an even more barbaric society. If you allow Adolf Hitler and the Nazis to seize control of a country and attack other countries with the advanced weaponry of the twentieth century, you may be forced into war. A rational civilization would have stopped the Nazis long before they had built the *Wehrmacht* into a terrifying instrument of conquest.

I strongly recommend not wasting time challenging the state or participating in futile political activity. No one can change the nature of the state into something benign. A state is defined by coercion. Institutional coercion is the principal source of the destructive forces of cultural decay. It has destroyed every great civilization of the past. Everything a state does is coercive and aims to reinforce the belief that it is necessary to maintain an advanced social order.

This leads to Juvenal's ultimate question: *"Sed quis custodiet ipsos custodes?"* But who will guard the guardians? All attempted political solutions to that conundrum have failed. Majority rule democracy is the current flavor. The thinking is that if we choose our rulers via periodic elections, they will be properly constrained to serving the people as some sort of philosopher-kings. However, political democracy always turns into mob rule, which means rule by the most ignorant. Hayek described in detail why the worst always get to the top in politics, whether in a democracy, monarchy, or dictatorship.[9] Keep in mind: The Athenian *demos* voted to kill Socrates. The Nazis gained power in the 1930s via elections.

The state is an unscientific bad idea. All states eventually decline and fall. There is no possible political system that can last. That includes all current democratic states. The American experiment in democracy will fail, if not through nuclear war, then through economic collapse brought about by accumulating, unpayable debt. The current US government has incurred more than $250 trillion of unfunded liabilities. Those are commitments politicians and bureaucrats have made to their citizens that are impossible to fulfill. The day of destruction is near.

No Longer in the Dark

We have not developed a truly scientific theory of volitional social systems until now because we have not incorporated the implications of the laws of thermodynamics at the most fundamental level of analysis. Until the mid-twentieth century, every social theorist had written about society at a great disadvantage. They were unaware of the importance of the laws of thermodynamics to our understanding of a prosperous civilization. This includes the great thinkers of the European Enlightenment: Baruch Spinoza, John Locke, David Hume, Adam Smith, Adam Ferguson, and the French philosophes and physiocrats François Quesnay, Voltaire, Denis Diderot, Nicolas de Condorcet, Turgot, and Étienne Bonnot de Condillac.

The most important eighteenth-century liberal was Thomas Paine, who, more than anyone else, created the intellectual basis of today's political systems. Paine originated the idea that the state exists to serve people rather than vice versa. He described the state as a necessary evil and a beast to be controlled at all costs.

Paine was a key founder of the United States. Jefferson, Washington, Franklin, and Adams admitted, sometimes grudgingly, in letters or public writings that his essay "Common Sense" convinced them to favor independence rather than reconciliation with the British crown. Paine was the one who suggested the new country be called the United States of America. As far as I know, he was the first person to advocate in writing for the abolition of slavery in an article published in 1775. He stated in clear, incendiary terms that it would be an abomination to allow the practice of African slavery to survive in the creation of a new country based on a right to life, liberty, and the pursuit of happiness. That same year, he wrote an article arguing that women should have the same rights as men.

Thomas Paine exerted more influence than any other intellectual on the liberal agenda of the Enlightenment, which led to the creation of the United States as the first country founded on a close approximation of freedom. We owe him a debt of gratitude that has yet to be properly expressed.

Although Paine was well-educated in Newtonian science, he died several decades before Sadi Carnot's discoveries, which led to the laws of thermodynamics. We now know that until people understand the second law, they will find it almost impossible to figure out the necessary characteristics of a social system capable of unlimited growth in perpetuity.

The laws of thermodynamics are probabilistic because of the constraints of evolutionary epistemology, the discipline describing how much or how little we can know about physical, biological, or volitional systems. As our knowledge increases, we will understand more about the physical systems beneath the statistical level we use to explain entropy. Scientific knowledge grows cumulatively. It develops more effective explanations over time. That depends, of course, on there being sufficient freedom to allow ongoing innovation.

The rise of cancel culture and the coercive enforcement of "the one true narrative" are not good omens.

Over the past three millennia, various Western civilizations have waxed and waned in cycles of growth and decay. Stronger customary property rights relative to other societies led to more prosperous cultures in Persia, Athens, and Rome. But it was the European Renaissance that gave birth to the Enlightenment and reached its zenith in the British Commonwealth and North America from the eighteenth to the twentieth centuries that produced our modern world with its high standard of living. As wealth accumulated in those cultures, it attracted hordes of parasitic thieves and their political witch doctors. They found that by stirring up envy, they could gain the approval of the masses and seize state power.

Why work hard to produce the things that make life better when you could steal the results of those who do? In a political democracy, you can then distribute the loot to the masses to win their support. H. L. Mencken said,

> The state ... consists of a gang of men exactly like you and me. They have, taking one with another, no special talent for the business of government; they have only a talent for getting and holding office. Their principal device to that end is to search out groups who pant and pine for something they can't get, and to promise to give it to them. Nine times out of ten that promise is worth nothing. The tenth time is made good by looting 'A' to satisfy 'B.' In other words, government

is a broker in pillage, and every election is a sort of advanced auction of stolen goods.[10]

There is a physical law called the law of least action that has an exact analog in the volitional world. Humans strive to get the most with the least effort. There are two ways to do that. One is innovation and high production; the other is to steal or mooch property from productive people. The first leads to vigorous growth. The second, particularly in the form of institutional theft, ends in destruction and extinction. This is why even the most prosperous cultures of the past eventually collapsed.

Until we develop innovative entrepreneurial ventures aimed at evolving beyond the state in the direction of freedom, we will be subject to coercive forces capable of destroying the civilization our ancestors worked so hard to create. Unless our intellectual and entrepreneurial leaders understand that a person's right to own the property he creates, including intellectual property, is crucial to survival, our future is in jeopardy. Ownership is the basis of freedom. If we don't evolve beyond our world of political coercion into a civilization with a far greater degree of freedom, we will remain in the dark. But if we see the light volitional science shines on the world, we will be on the verge of a magnificent cosmic expansion.

Let's get on with it!

★   ★   ★

Recap

- The first and second laws of thermodynamics are the most important physical laws affecting the behavior of all living organisms. The second law states that energy flows from orderly to disorderly, higher-entropy states. Entropy is roughly a measure of disorder in the universe.

- The tendency of energy to flow from concentrated, orderly states to more disorderly, higher-entropy states erodes and destroys the physical and social infrastructures of intelligent beings. Living organisms must constantly exert effort to preserve their biochemical order. Likewise, volitional beings must constantly work to build and maintain a civilization that can expand into the cosmos indefinitely.

- Humans cooperate to build institutional structures that will protect us from the destructive forces of entropy. The only realistic way to ensure the cooperation necessary to counteract entropy is through markets, which are cooperative social systems arising from noncoercive property exchanges seeking mutual profit. Profit is a natural measure of how well innovators and entrepreneurs are using available resources to serve others.

- Volitional science asserts that secure property boundaries are as important for society as cell walls are for organic life. They allow humans to cooperate and thus create, discover, and build things that make our social systems more resilient.

- Primary (intangible) property is the most valuable property. Creating and disseminating primary property is the basis of all progress. The human imagination is the source of all other property. People create secondary (tangible) property by conceiving ideas or using someone else's ideas to produce new products.

- Capitalism emerges from free markets. It resists entropy by motivating people to create, build, and expand the physical and social structures of civilization. In contrast, political systems increase local entropy by supporting coercion and violence instead of peaceful cooperation.

- Don't waste time challenging the state or participating in political activity. No one can change the nature of the state into something benign. Everything a state does is coercive and reinforces the mistaken belief that a state is necessary to maintain an advanced civilization. The state is an unscientific, bad idea that does not work, thus it cannot last.

6

Volitional Beings and Cultural Evolution

*The way in which these streams of human culture
flow is gradual, incremental, undirected, emergent
and driven by natural selection among competing
ideas. . . . And though it has no goal in mind, cultural evolution nonetheless produces functional and
ingenious solutions to problems—what biologists
call adaptation.*

—Matt Ridley

LOGIC AND CAUSE-EFFECT REASONING are innate
mental attributes shaping how we develop knowledge. Various combinations of the two are the best way to format and
transmit useful information about the world. Both abilities
evolved over several million years in early proto-humans,
along with five additional generic cognitive abilities Ludwig von Mises identified as essential components of human
intelligence (see below). The entities resulting from this singular evolutionary pathway are as different from mere living

organisms as life is from inanimate systems of matter and energy. Thus, we designate a new category of natural phenomena, of which humans are the only known example: **volitional beings**.

Volitional Beings

Volition is the ability to assess different courses of action and choose one to pursue. Intelligence is included in the term *volition*. Intelligence can only emerge in a being with a survival instinct that evolves into an ability to make choices in pursuit of survival and happiness. The ability of volitional beings to cooperate via voluntary exchange (markets) ratcheted that pursuit to a more effective level. It gave rise to social systems governed by an underlying natural order to which we must adjust our actions to survive and prosper. Fortunately for us, these market systems are precisely those that maximize individual liberty.

Ludwig von Mises identified six innate cognitive attributes necessary for human action.[1] We can generalize them into universal qualities required for any being to be capable of volitional action. Each distinct attribute depends upon and may share qualities with the other five. They form an overlapping, integrated whole.

A volitional being must possess:

- **An awareness of temporality:** Volitional beings are aware of the flow of time. They are aware of the past, present, and future.
- **Causality and logic:** Volitional beings organize the

input they perceive through their senses in cause-effect and logical relationships. They use that ability to pursue their goals.

- **An awareness of uncertainty:** Volitional beings know their knowledge of the world is limited and that there is an outer boundary beyond which they are ignorant. They know they don't know the future with certainty. The innate awareness of uncertainty motivates them to strive to reduce their ignorance.

- **Constant, recurrent dissatisfaction:** Volitional beings experience dissatisfaction that can never be satiated. Dissatisfaction is the motivation for all action. Without it, there could be no purposeful human action.

- **The ability to imagine a preferred state of affairs:** Volitional beings can conceive of a hypothetical condition they would prefer to their present condition. That's the necessary complement to dissatisfaction. What people prefer derives from their subjective frame of reference.

- **An awareness of means:** Volitional beings must have beliefs or expectations about means they can use to satisfy their wants. They can perceive ways of acting they believe will enable them to transition from their current condition to what they presume will be better.

Volition is the ability to choose. Intelligent beings capable of volitional action gradually emerged during the six million years after hominids diverged from other primates. Our ancestors evolved into beings who could choose between different courses of action based on a rational but imperfect assessment of anticipated gains and losses. Thus, a volitional being is a living organism pursuing meaningful goals guided by rationality and beliefs, however mistaken, about how the world works.

Every action involves a choice. To act means individuals choose ends from the set of those they value most and select the means to pursue those ends. The means usually involve steps they may modify based on information gained along the way. They may also change the ends they are seeking. For volitional beings, life is a continuous series of choices.

Subjective Value

In the seventeenth through nineteenth centuries, classical economists were stumped by a fundamental problem involving how people value goods. Adam Smith described it this way:

> The things which have the greatest value in use have frequently little or no value in exchange; and, on the contrary, those which have the greatest value in exchange have frequently little or no value in use. Nothing is more useful than water: but it will purchase scarce any thing; scarce any thing can be had in exchange for it. A diamond, on the contrary, has scarce any value in use; but a very great quantity of other goods may frequently be had in exchange for it.[2]

If everyone recognizes water is far more useful than diamonds, why do diamonds command a much higher price? In the first forty pages of *The Wealth of Nations*, Smith explained the problem with a series of confused, disconnected analyses in which he concluded that the value of goods derives from the labor it took to produce them.

The problem with this explanation is that experience exposes it as flat wrong. Value does not derive, as Smith and Marx believed, from the quantity of labor it takes to produce something. Nor does it arise, as other classical writers supposed, from a good's cost of production or any quality inherent in goods. People pay a high price for diamonds for various reasons involving vanity, status, and what they believe to be true love. (See the endnotes for an example that explodes the fallacy once and for all.[3]) Water is cheap compared to almost everything else because it is abundant. Our planet is drowning in it.

In 1871, Carl Menger, founder of the Austrian School of Economics, disclosed the theory of subjective value and the counterintuitive idea of marginal utility in his revolutionary work *Principles of Economics.*[4] Thinkers as far back as Aristotle and a school of fifteenth- and sixteenth-century Spanish scholastic philosophers had discussed value as a subjective notion. But until Menger, no one had elucidated it or used it as the basis of economic theory.

According to Menger, value is subjective to each separate individual.

When I discussed the nature of value, I observed that value is nothing inherent in goods and that it is not a property of goods. But neither is value an independent thing. There is no reason why a good may not have value

139

to one economizing individual but no value to another individual under different circumstances. The *measure* of value is entirely subjective in nature, and for this reason a good can have great value to one economizing individual, little value to another, and no value at all to a third, depending upon the differences in their requirements and available amounts [of the good in question]. What one person disdains or values lightly is appreciated by another, and what one person abandons is often picked up by another. While one economizing individual esteems equally a given amount of one good and a greater amount of another good, we frequently observe just the opposite evaluations with another economizing individual.

Hence not only the *nature* but also the *measure* of value is subjective. Goods always have value to certain economizing individuals and this value is also *determined* only by these individuals.[5]

Menger realized the source of value lies in an individual's preferences and inclinations as constrained by his material circumstances. That may seem an obvious insight with few theoretical implications. Yet, it turned out to be the basis of a powerful theory leading to better explanations of all aspects of the socioeconomic world.

Menger explained that value derives from an individual's desires being unlimited while the resources available to satisfy those desires are limited or, in economic terms, scarce. Our scarcest resource is time; we are mortal. This conflict between unlimited wants and limited resources leads us to compute preferences. We compare and evaluate the things we desire and, in so doing, automatically create an ordinal list of preferences derived from those evaluations.

It is important to recognize our scale of preferences changes as conditions change, and our wants can never be fully satiated. As soon as we attain one desired end, new desires always emerge.

Menger established that the source of value and prices lies in each person's assessment of the means available to attain their most valued ends. In a market economy, prices are an ever-changing number that integrates the results of all interactions into a useful measure, signaling the availability of everything with economic value, including human skills, talents, and knowledge. In his effort to make economics a science, Menger developed the epistemology of methodological individualism, which is the basis of our approach to volitional science.[6]

Axiom of Action

During the first half of the twentieth century, Menger's student Ludwig von Mises took a significant further step. Mises realized the theory of subjective value explained how acts of exchange determine prices on commercial markets. It was also the fount, not just of economic action but of *all* action. He extended and deepened Menger's epistemology into a general science of human action based on what Mises called the "axiom of action," which he considered a generic description of human action: "Action means the employment of means to attain ends. It is an attempt to substitute a more satisfactory state of affairs for a less satisfactory one. We call such an induced alteration an exchange. A less desirable condition is bartered for one more desirable. What gratifies less is abandoned to attain something that pleases more."[7]

Mises agreed with the Declaration of Independence on the fundamental importance of pursuing happiness. There's no valid objection to a usage that defines human action as the striving for happiness.

All human actions can be understood as the pursuit of happiness. Mises defined happiness as "an individual's subjective preferences." He used the axiom of action as the fundamental postulate of a theory of human action, from which he derived the theorems and principles of economics, including incisive explanations of how markets work, the role of entrepreneurs, and why the effects of political intervention end up being the opposite of those intended.

The error of all nonsubjective theories of value is to think one can arrive at an objective measure or procedure for calculating the value of economic goods, or anything else for that matter. We each seek what we consider "good" and avoid what we regard as "bad" according to our own idiosyncratic system of values. Our values do not map one-to-one onto anyone else's values. Each person's system of values is unique. No one can determine what someone else should value or whether the evaluation behind someone's action is good or bad, right or wrong.

Only the person who chooses an action is in a position to determine if he's satisfied with how things turned out. What makes anything preferable depends on each person's subjective values. Profit-seeking entrepreneurs must appeal to those tastes or go out of business. Financial profit measures how well a business serves its customers.

An entrepreneur may try to guide his customers to what he believes are more aspirational goods, but only through voluntary persuasion. Markets work effectively to manufacture and deliver ever higher quality goods and services that people want because markets align with the reality of human nature and the broader world of physical and biological reality.

Uniqueness corollary: No two volitional beings have identical values.

Many people may buy the same shirt on a given day because it is fashionable. Millions of people may watch the same TV shows or movies. Most prefer health to illness, more money to less. If many people share the same preferences simultaneously, it does not contradict the assertion that each person's motivations, values, and preferences are unique. Those differences make the world go round. The enormous variety of abilities and skills underpins the effectiveness of the division of labor and Ricardo's law of association, which shows that it's always more profitable for an advanced culture to engage in voluntary trade with a more primitive culture than to enslave them. The fact that everyone's values are subjective and idiosyncratic is the foundation of all exchange. People cooperate to exchange property in ways they believe will improve their lives according to their unique values.

Transaction: A voluntary exchange of property between volitional beings.

Transaction principle: Every transaction between two or more volitional beings results from the different value each party places on the property being exchanged.

It is a common misconception that a transaction occurs when two people agree on the value of what is being exchanged. A higher voodoo version is that exchanges occur because of some hypothetical objective exchange equivalence. Economists are led astray by physics envy into static notions such as exchange equivalence and equilibrium, but in capitalism, economic reality is never static. Equilibrium is an imaginary condition under which no action could occur because everyone has exhausted all possible avenues of exchange. Their every desire has been satisfied. The only correlate in reality is death.

Equilibrium is a useful idea in economics. It is an imaginary ideal used in *Gedanken* experiments (thought experiments) to understand how markets work. The mistake is to assert that satisfying current desires is the end of the story. The moment people get what they think will bring them greater happiness, they begin pursuing other ends. Happiness is an ever-receding goal. It can never be fully attained.

Energy, Disorder, and Order
Volition evolved out of the primitive purpose we call the survival instinct exhibited by even the simplest one-celled

144

organisms. A living organism is a system of organized matter and energy pursuing survival by accessing energy flowing down natural thermodynamic gradients. It applies that energy to assemble and maintain its organizational integrity in the face of destructive physical and biological forces.

According to the latest explanations, life appeared 3.5 to 4 billion years ago around thermal vents rising from the ocean floor. Semi-stable systems of chemical reactions appeared, fueled by energy flowing out of the vents. Those chemical systems used nearby molecules, mineral catalysts, and heat energy from the Earth's core to assemble and maintain increasingly complex forms of organization by physical laws alone.

At some point, that led to lipid boundaries, which provided a protective barrier against the natural forces undermining life's order. When the primitive lipid barrier evolved into a cell wall, the chemical precursors of metabolism were subjected to evolutionary forces that gave rise to more complex organisms over several billion years. All living organisms must access energy to power the internal biochemical reactions that support the integrity of cellular operations. They are constantly building, repairing, replicating, ejecting waste, and seeking new energy sources to survive for as long as possible.

In physical terms, such systems of concentrated energy and matter are thermodynamically unstable and prone to disintegrate in the absence of external energy supplies. The physical world exerts constant pressure on all living and nonliving systems to break down and disperse into less orderly states. But life moves in the opposite direction; its purpose is to survive. Living organisms strive to maintain an orderly system within an identifiable material boundary. They do so without violating the laws of thermodynamics because life exists as an open system exposed to constant energy flows from the external universe. For example, our biosphere feeds off solar radiation and stored energy rising from the Earth's core. Living systems tap into those energy flows to build and preserve their local organization.

In doing so, they accelerate the production of entropy in the universe. Thus, life's ability to create order (negative entropy) pushes the universe into a higher-entropy state than it would have been without the emergence of life. That's not a worry. The universe is vast and mostly empty. And in a free civilization, our knowledge will constantly expand in ways we cannot imagine. According to David Deutsch, volitional beings are universal explainers and constructors. Since acquirable knowledge is infinite and open-ended, we will, at some future point when we are no longer constrained by bureaucratic intervention, solve the waste/entropy problem in a way that leads to an ongoing flowstream of ever-better solutions.

Darwinian evolution has produced organisms of greater complexity over large stretches of time through a bottom-up trial-and-error process. Each new generation of genetic variants competed against other organisms for access to finite resources. Given the environment and available resources, the most successful variants survived and reproduced in greater numbers. At some point in our evolutionary history, certain cells joined together by chemical laws and biological processes (e.g., predation, as when certain cells consumed other cells, and the prey remained intact to become the mitochondria that power the cells of every organism today). These cells sublimated their individual survival to the survival of the organism of which they were now a component. This conferred a huge survival advantage, and these more complex organisms eventually came to dominate the planet.

But enhanced survival came with a cost. Living systems of greater complexity needed access to more energy than simpler organisms to maintain their structure, replicate, and survive. That's why life forms, including us, strive to access external energy flows to survive and prosper. The challenge for living organisms is that as energy becomes more dispersed and gradients disappear, it becomes unusable. For any closed system, thermodynamic equilibrium is a condition in which the system's energy has been maximally dispersed, and no work can be done. For a living organism, that means death and, unless a species can continually access energy from external sources, extinction.

The great advantage conferred by intelligence is we can develop a deeper scientific understanding of life and apply it to maintain the integrity of our cells and bodies far beyond our current lifespans. By further developing our understanding of physics, biology, and volitional science, we can create more effective tools to access new energy sources.

The flow of energy in the physical universe in the direction of greater randomness and disorder is the context that gives purpose to life and shapes the survival strategies organisms have evolved. The energy gradients giving birth to life and providing the fuel to upgrade its structural vigor are the same ones that relentlessly eat away at and destroy its organization. Brahma, Vishnu, and Shiva in one package.

In this case, what's true in the biological domain is true in the social domain. The death of a civilization is analogous to the death of a person or the extinction of a species. Societies die when coercion overwhelms their organizational integrity. The most dangerous form of coercion is state or institutional coercion. Every prior significant culture collapsed from either (1) states interfering in markets so forcefully that society's productive vigor was overwhelmed, leading to poverty and deprivation, or (2) state monopolies of justice and security failed to protect productive citizens from external and internal barbarians, resulting in widespread criminality and chaos.

Biological Versus Cultural Evolution

The appearance of intelligent volitional beings signaled a new entity governed by a new set of natural laws that are different from, but not contradictory to, the laws of the physical and biological worlds. What follows is the most plausible explanation I've found of how self-aware intelligence may have evolved. Our knowledge of the six-million-year period of evolution producing modern humans is too meager to provide a verifiable account of how it happened. Despite that, when such an account is rendered, it will be close to the following hypothetical just-so story.[8]

The striving of living systems to survive is what distinguishes the biological realm from nonliving physical systems. But there's more. Life at every level was subjected to a relentless evolution that resulted in organisms of ever-greater organizational complexity. Per the second law, mere physical systems always degrade into less orderly states of lower complexity.

The attribute of life that triggered the later stages of Darwin-Wallace evolution is the ability of organisms to produce copies of themselves that incorporate novel traits in a few of their offspring. Within the context of the long-term stability of the biosphere, life allows for the occasional appearance of novelty. Over time, a few offspring (phenotypes) are born with genes that enhance their ability to survive and reproduce. Sexual reproduction accelerates that process by creating offspring, each with its unique genetic pattern, allowing for even greater phenotypical variety.

Biological evolution is characterized by non-teleological, contingent progress toward greater organizational complexity. It has produced organisms possessing a greater ability to survive, reproduce, and dominate the planet. Over 3.5 billion years, it has created the increasingly complex biosphere, both supportive of life and deadly, from which humans emerged.

Evolution's power derives from ruthless competition and occasional unthinking cooperation among members of the same and different species for the resources each needs to survive. Winners are the variants possessing traits that enable them to survive and reproduce in greater numbers. Per Tennyson, the living world is "red in tooth and claw." Evolution also discovered cells could join in organisms of greater complexity, enabling them to better deal with the challenges of survival. Cells sacrificed their autonomy for a more effective means of survival.

Cultural evolution differs from biological evolution at this point. It relies on free markets, and as Jay Snelson noted, "A free market is biological evolution minus coercion." I would rephrase it as "biological evolution minus violence." Animals cannot coerce because they cannot understand property or morality.

Over time, biological competition honed and intensified the genetically encoded survival instinct in individual organisms. But none has yet escaped death. Entropic decay gets them in the end. Early on, life evolved reproduction to get around the problem of death, but for individual organisms, the outcome remained the same. Everyone dies. Either they end up as food (fuel) for predatory organisms, or they succumb to the wear and tear of relentless dissipative forces. Since death is ubiquitous, it must serve a deep evolutionary purpose. By clearing out organisms once they've reproduced, it frees up finite resources for new generations. No fundamental law of nature that we know of implies an organism cannot maintain its organizational integrity and survive indefinitely. Death was such a powerful driver of progress that biological evolution became dependent on it.

It's just the opposite with cultural evolution. In a robust capitalist civilization, death is antithetical to progress. Advanced forms of capitalism will depend on the knowledge and experience of people living for thousands of years in youthful bodies. Death will no longer be a driver of progress but an obstacle to overcome. It will take innovators operating in free markets to develop the scientific knowledge and derivative technologies to make long, youthful lifespans a reality.

Biological evolution made this a possibility when it gave birth to volitional beings with self-awareness and intelligence.

Naysayers, obstructionists, and religious fanatics whose belief systems depend on death won't be able to stop the onset of long lifespans. Those who accept death as an unalterable fact of life will be seen as members of a primitive cult. And, of course, in a cosmic civilization, they will be free to die if they so choose.

The markets of the future will generate incentives that put such a premium on innovation that people living for thousands of years, rather than being a hindrance, will use their accumulating knowledge and wisdom to supercharge progress.

Evolution of Volitional Intelligence

The precursor of volition appeared when certain animals evolved limbic systems with primitive emotions. Emotions act as signals that intensify and guide an organism's will to survive. Once our hominid ancestors diverged from the primates, they entered a unique evolutionary process in which the survival instinct governed by primitive limbic feedback developed into full-fledged volitional intelligence.

We don't know the timing or the specific mechanisms by which it happened, but British neuroscientist Raymond Tallis developed a hypothetical explanation I find the most plausible. He believed the key to developing self-awareness, consciousness, and rationality was the coevolution of four things: hominid neurological systems, bipedalism, powerful stereoscopic visual acuity, and prehensile hands with opposable thumbs. He speculated that human-level intelligence evolved from our bipedal, upright prehuman ancestors using their prehensile hands to do things no animal had ever done. They used those marvelous hands to grasp and manipulate things in their environment, which became toolmaking. Toolmaking is the beginning of culture. It is a skill passed down to new generations, a knowledge that accumulates and advances.[9]

Tallis focused on the abilities that differentiate humans from other animals and how those differences may have developed. His analysis parallels Richard Dawkins's hypothetical explanation in *The Blind Watchmaker* of how such a complex sense organ as the human eye might have evolved from primitive photoreceptors by Darwinian means. As Tallis explained, rational intelligence must have evolved gradually because that's how biological evolution works and because the first beings with incipient rationality needed time to adapt to its requirements. In the precarious world of early hominids, when a predator leaped out of the bushes on the savannah, an instinctual response honed over millions of years would work better for survival than stopping to reason about how to react.

Further evidence favoring the gradual emergence of volitional intelligence is that our prehuman ancestors did not develop a spoken language, as useful as it has proven to be, until around a hundred thousand years ago. Writing, the symbolic representation of spoken language in a physical format, only appeared around five to ten thousand years ago. In other words, after the first hominids diverged from primates, six million years elapsed before they developed a symbolic language.

Cultural evolution moves far faster than biological evolution, and the acquisition of a symbolic language accelerated its progress by orders of magnitude. One or two millennia after our ancestors produced the first primitive forms of writing, they developed an alphabet to form words, sentences, and messages. They began expressing these messages in durable media (stone tablets, papyrus, etc.) so their stories, explanations, and wisdom could be passed on to future generations. They also used language and logic to develop arithmetic skills, a powerful measurement tool. In sum, they could now store and accumulate knowledge in permanent form.

It seems obvious that acute stereoscopic vision would provide an advantage to any being who possessed it. Yet there's more to it than meets the eye, so to speak. But why would Tallis focus on bipedalism and the prehensile hand to explain the evolution of intelligence? First, it seems likely all three traits evolved together because each becomes more powerful when integrated with the other two. Bipedalism gives a being an elevated, broader view of the world and frees up two of his four feet as hands he can use to probe and manipulate things. Doing so would activate a feedback loop between his hands and his most important sensory system, the eye, and its associated cognitive visual processing. To this day, we consider a person who exhibits unusually dexterous hand-eye coordination to possess a distinct advantage in accomplishing almost any task.

As these first hominids began using their hands to craft primitive tools, they also developed an elementary form of explanatory knowledge to teach others how to make them. They were evolving beyond the instinctual, range-bound behavior of other animals. Even the most advanced mammals

153

don't seem to be aware they are unique creatures distinct from other members of their kind. Animals are submerged in their environment. They are immersed in a world of smells, sounds, and sights to which they react instinctually. Volitional beings, alone, can use their imagination to stand outside of and differentiate themselves from their environment. It was only in the hominid ancestors of today's humans that the instinctual urge to survive evolved over several million years into volitional intelligence.

Early hominids began using their hands to point out things—a poisonous snake or an edible plant—to other members of the tribe, further reinforcing the budding realization each exists as a separate being with a separate point of viewing the world. They began to think in prelinguistic forms of "me and you," "us and them," and "he and she." They were becoming self-aware and were beginning to think of rudimentary categories: "me and everyone (or everything) else."

When someone points to something, he is pointing it out to someone else. That implies the pointer is aware other people have a different viewpoint than he does. Prelinguistic pointing implies the pointer is aware he can see something others may not see because they have a different point of view. The act of pointing further reinforces self-awareness and individuation. The path to cooperation is now wide open.

When proto-humans began pointing out things to each other, making more sophisticated tools, sharing their knowledge with other members of the tribe, and passing it on for the benefit of progeny, they happened upon the greatest means ever discovered to enhance their survival and improve their ability to pursue happiness. Voluntary cooperation with others was the sign they had stumbled into culture.

That's when cultural evolution, which had developed alongside and was intertwined with biological evolution, got traction. Meanwhile, biological evolution, operating through genes, continued selecting physical traits, a few of which accelerated cultural evolution, e.g., a larger frontal lobe, particularly the prefrontal cortex. These two parallel evolutionary systems, cultural and biological, spawned powerful feedback loops between them that acted over myriad generations to drive the selection of ever more complex neurological systems, the biophysical substrate necessary for more advanced communication and cooperation.

Cooperation

Cultural evolution results from cooperation. Ironically, it only surfaces when people realize each is a separate, discrete being who can be distinguished from other members of their kind. Self-awareness stems from the realization we can look at our environment and find means to better pursue survival and greater happiness in our own way. We begin seeing ourselves as individuals with our own viewpoints and agendas, distinct from everyone else's. Over time, that realization becomes embedded because, ironically, it fosters cooperation, which enhances the security and survival of the tribe and its members.

Individuals have different abilities and perspectives. When they apply them in cooperation with others, they open new, more sophisticated means of ensuring survival and pursuing happiness. Simple markets emerged when people became aware the members of their tribe and nearby tribes possessed skills they could access by working together through agreements and property exchanges. Of course, people and tribes also got things through violence and the threat of violence. Violence is the opposite of cooperation and self-extinguishes over time because people ultimately find it less profitable. Cooperation through markets is the great driving force of cultural progress.

Once primitive humans developed a symbolic language, cultural evolution powered by their cumulative knowledge of the world became irreversible. It inexorably began to overtake biological evolution as the most powerful driver of progress. Progress is a subjective idea to which each person may attribute a different meaning. When a culture produces knowledge that accumulates and leads to technologies enhancing survivability, it supports larger numbers of people in a standard of living that most, by their choices, prefer. The outcomes of cultural evolution are contingent on personal decisions and are only predictable in general terms. Once early humans discovered the efficacy of cooperation through markets, they entered the era of cultural evolution that has the possibility of becoming irreversible once we fully understand the power of noncoercive markets.

★ ★ ★

Recap

- Volitional beings are a new life form that emerged from the biological world, just as life emerged from the physical world.

- The volitional domain is governed by natural laws that don't apply to the physical and biological domains. However, the natural laws governing the volitional world cannot contradict or violate the natural laws of the lower-level domains.

- The appearance of volitional beings led to cultural evolution, a new, more powerful evolutionary system that, like biological evolution, is open-ended, adaptive, non-teleological, and evolved in a bottom-up manner, leading to greater organizational complexity.

- Humans learned to cooperate when they realized they were unique individuals with a point of view different from others of their kind. Self-awareness and individuation led to cooperation and cultural evolution, which intensified the evolution of the more complex neurological systems necessary for volition, consciousness, rationality, and linguistic communication. The most valuable result is the development of markets in ideas that have produced the cumulative knowledge we call science.

- Cultural evolution differs from biological evolution at the most fundamental level. Biological evolution has no way for the individual organism to escape extinction. A market civilization with sufficiently strong property rights can reach civilizational escape velocity and enter an irreversible growth phase that can last for the duration of the cosmos.

- Volitional beings must exert effort to survive the inexorable energy flow toward greater randomness and homogeneity. Without such effort abetted by scientific innovation and profit-seeking companies, civilization will succumb to entropy and become extinct.

- Voluntary cooperation (markets) is the most effective means for enhancing human survival and prosperity. Markets based on property rights will nurture and protect people who discover better ways to work together in pursuing happiness. Such markets give rise to sustained scientific and technological progress that entrepreneurs turn into goods and services to protect civilization from entropy's destructive wear and tear.

7

Compensation for Scientific and Other Innovations

If the problem is real, then the people who are best at solving the problem at hand should rise to the top. That is not power. It is the authority that properly accompanies ability.

—Jordan Peterson

NEW IDEAS AND EXPLANATIONS originate in the minds of individual innovators. They submit their ideas to qualified peers for criticism, improvement, testing, and application in technological devices, products, and services. The ultimate test of the truth and value of an idea is how effectively and broadly it is applied in products and services sold in markets. A rough measure of the importance of an idea is the cumulative value of what it makes possible, particularly in markets of voluntary exchange.

How could evolutionary markets deal with the ownership of scientific and other innovations? Is there a pragmatic and just way to treat the most valuable and consequential property humans create—the universal theories, natural laws, mathematical methods, and equations we call science? If we can achieve that, we can easily handle the less important tangible property with the same general principles.

Problems and Questions

There are two general problems in dealing with the ownership of scientific knowledge, the solutions of which will coalesce into an integrated approach as we evolve into a sustainable civilization.

1. Individuals who are no longer alive developed much of the scientific knowledge we use today. But, volitional science asserts that the ownership of primary property is perpetual. If the owner is dead, how can he license his work and collect royalties for its use?
2. Innovators will continue to develop valuable new knowledge for as long as civilization exists. How can we deal with the ownership and compensation of current and future innovation? Can we create noncoercive market systems for registering, protecting, disseminating, and compensating intellectual property?

To properly understand the following explanations, let go of preconceptions from your lifelong immersion in a coercive political world and, while never straying from a pragmatic adherence to reality, imagine a different kind of social system that could accomplish two basic goals: market justice for intellectual innovators, and a dynamic civilization of maximal freedom and creativity. In such a civilization, the possibility of chaos or collapse would decrease to zero, and innovation and creativity would flourish as never before.

In chapter 2, we considered three categories of property:

1. Primordial property (P-zero): One's physical body.
2. Primary property (P1): One's intangible creations (theories, ideas, stories, songs, etc.), a.k.a. intellectual property.
3. Secondary property (P2): One's tangible creations (financial assets, cars, tables, etc.).

When it comes to intellectual property (P1), is ownership morally desirable? Does it accord with justice? Will it lead to a more prosperous civilization? How could the owner-creators of intangible theories, natural laws, and mathematical innovations be compensated without strangling the free flow of information? For example, if the creator of a scientific theory owns it, what happens if he refuses to license its use?

It will help in understanding the systems developed here if we keep a few things in mind. If progress in biological science continues without interruption, we will at some point develop indefinitely long, youthful lifespans. Intellectual property (IP) systems must derive from universally valid principles that apply to past, nonliving innovators and future innovators living in civilizations of effectively immortal people. There needs to be continuity of those basic principles from the past into the future because, theoretically, once a post-political civilization achieves stabilized durable growth, it could last as long as the universe. Our progeny a hundred thousand years hence will view Archimedes, Newton, Einstein, and those of us alive today as having lived in the same era. By including past non-living innovators, we are doing what Newton did when he asserted that gravitation was a universal force that existed everywhere in the universe. Until the publication of the *Principia*, most people had assumed two separate realms: Earth and everything else.

To understand the IP systems presented here, I suggest one adopt the far longer timescales used in volitional science. Including nonliving innovators in IP registration, dissemination, and compensation accords with justice. It is pragmatic because it can easily evolve into an advanced culture of indefinitely long lifespans and productive individuals who assess their actions in far longer time frames.

A Theory of Compensation

Why do we compensate anyone for anything? The answer in volitional science is gratitude.

> **Gratitude:** The market acknowledgment, where due, for value received.

Since value is determined by the one who receives something, only the user, licensee, or consumer can set the price of a product, including scientific theories. That seems wrong at first glance because, in today's world, the seller sets the price of everyday items for the consumer's convenience. Most of us don't want to haggle over the cost of goods each time we purchase them. But even in that situation, the consumer implicitly sets the price by buying or not buying. The ultimate form of consumer protection is the right not to buy at the offered price.

In a free market, if producers do not offer a price acceptable to consumers, their products won't sell. Producers analyze consumer feedback and adjust prices to achieve the highest realistic profits. Market competition drives them to offer products of ever higher quality at ever lower prices. In free markets, producers are servants of consumers.

Regarding primary property,[1] how would entrepreneurs decide what to pay innovators in a way that is convenient and reasonable? Galambos's ingenious solution was that all ideas would be registered with private registration companies that verified ownership (see natural estates below). These companies would then publish databases of ideas open to the public for a nominal fee or perhaps no fee. Anyone could search these databases via search algorithms for ideas useful to their business or research institute. Anyone could use any idea under two unmistakably clear conditions: (1) no coercive use and (2) payment of a non-zero royalty. To be clear, no one is mandating those terms. They are simply Galambos's educated guess as to what sort of terms would be most profitable for both innovators and those who license the use of their ideas.

The first condition means you may not use ideas to produce weapons to kill and destroy. It further implies that no state agent would be permitted to use any of the theories, ideas, or inventions of modern physical or biological science. The second condition follows from the brief explanation above about who sets prices. Be forewarned; it runs counter to today's economic thinking.

Anyone who agrees to these conditions will have unimpeded access to use any idea in the registered databases. It would be like a giant vending machine in the cloud offering scientific and technical ideas to anyone willing to accept the two terms above. In a free market, companies would offer specialized searches for a fee. If, for instance, a research institute licensed an idea or an entire set of ideas, those ideas would be available to every researcher who worked with the institute. I expect there would be scouts who would make a very profitable living by seeking out new ideas and making them known to appropriate scientists, innovators, and entrepreneurs. Nothing would prevent the open publication of any new idea or experiment. Innovators would be free to handle the usage of their ideas any way they wished. However, for those who chose to offer their ideas under the two terms above, the only difference would be a proviso pointing potential licensees to the innovator's registration company.

If a registration company certified ownership of an idea in the name of the wrong person, they would be liable for the error and suffer a loss of reputation and future business unless they quickly rectified it. They would also be responsible for paying restitution for financial damage. Private insurance companies would insure against such errors for a premium. The premium paid for such insurance would be a matter of public record. A lower premium would signal a more competent registration company.

Payment of a non-zero royalty at an amount set by the licensee gives entrepreneurs a maximal incentive to use any idea to produce products and services at prices that accord with profit optimization. They would only pay a royalty on revenue generated by products in which the idea was used, the amount being at the user's sole discretion. Innovators could handle their ideas any way they wished. They could charge a large up-front access fee, but that would be counterproductive. In freedom, however, no one will be forced to do anything, including things that might be more financially profitable.

Who would determine the amount of a royalty and the party to whom it should be paid? Each corporation, entrepreneur, or other user would determine the royalty amount. What they pay would be a matter of public record. The criterion used is simple. It would be the royalty, or range of royalties, for all the IP they applied in their products that optimized long-term profits. Remember, profit measures how effectively entrepreneurs and businesses provide value to their customers.

One objection to full IP rights is that if IP ownership is perpetual and cannot be sold or transferred, then dead people own ideas in perpetuity. That sounds absurd; it means the dead hand of the past could put a damper on innovation going forward. For example, if Isaac Newton owned his ideas in perpetuity, how could someone like an obscure patent clerk in Berne, Switzerland, get permission from Newton to use his work? Without access to Newtonian science, the entire infrastructure of modern civilization would not have been possible. Who would register Newton's, Maxwell's, or Archimedes's ideas under the above conditions? Who would license their use?

The Natural Estate

The solution is a new entity called the **natural estate**. It is called that because everyone has one by virtue of their existence as a volitional being. Each person's natural estate begins at birth and lasts forever. It's the cumulative store and record of achievements throughout their lives.

> **Natural estate:** The totality of all property that accrues to people during their lives and thereafter. It is the cumulative store and record in perpetuity of the achievements and property they have created.

Most people live within a short-term time frame and accomplish little of lasting value. There is nothing wrong with that. It does not make someone bad or non-useful. Civilization needs pharmacists, dry cleaners, car salesmen, plumbers, lab technicians, etc., just as much as it needs scientific innovators. However, certain people like Archimedes, Newton, and Maxwell have produced intellectual property that increases in value every year and will do so for as long as civilization lasts. If these three men were to receive a vanishingly small royalty (e.g., 0.00001 percent) from the revenue all entrepreneurs generated worldwide from applying their ideas to products and services, their natural estates would be among the world's largest accumulations of wealth.

A natural estate is a perpetual financial entity set up to register ownership and receive compensation for an individual's work. The innovators mentioned above are dead; who would manage their natural estates? In most of today's world, setting up such a perpetual financial trust is illegal. But in a more enlightened civilization, there would be no state to make anything illegal. The idea of the natural estate assumes we have evolved beyond today's barbaric world in which many potentially valuable things are illegal and suppressed. In the future, the only thing to be suppressed (and suppressed without resort to coercion) will be any action involving coercion.

Newton's natural estate would probably be the largest accumulation of private capital in civilization. I will use it as an example. But before I do, let me address you, the reader. If you were to create something of lasting value, how would you like to be paid for it even a thousand years from now? What I'm describing could apply to you as well as Newton.

The first question is, who would manage it? Newton did not leave a will appointing a trustee for his natural estate nor instructions for how it should be managed because he was unaware of such a concept. The solution is that managers would be selected via a competitive market process. Anyone could set up a natural estate for Newton and claim it as the rightful place to receive royalties from all the entrepreneurs and research institutes who use Newton's ideas to make products and services, including new scientific theories. There could be many such claimants to represent his estate. Markets are brutally effective at separating wheat from chaff. No competent entrepreneur would pay royalties to an incompetent estate manager. All claimants representing Newton's estate would be winnowed naturally and noncoercively to very few, perhaps eventually getting down to one or two. There would be nothing to keep competing trusts from merging into one.

If market competition yielded only one natural estate for Newton, some might cry monopoly. They could claim that due to Newton's vast importance, his trust could exert a malign influence over the entire culture. If a monopoly is the singular ownership and control of an economic or commercial entity, innovators automatically have a monopoly on the ideas, products, and services they create. In free markets, that's not a problem; it's a solution. The only problematic monopoly is one enforced by legal coercion, such as today's state monopolies on issuing currency, providing justice, and securing national defense.

What if Newton's estate decided to restrict the use of his ideas to white supremacists or red-headed Scots between the ages of thirty-five and fifty-five? Or what if they demanded high licensing rates few could afford? Making such onerous conditions would be irrational and stupid. It would severely decrease the royalty revenue and limit Newton's positive effect on civilization. This would impact the estate managers' compensation, which would be directly tied to the value of their capital assets. The negative market response triggered by restricting access to an innovator's ideas in any way other than the two conditions given above—no coercive use and payment of a non-zero royalty—would lead entrepreneurs to look elsewhere for estate licensing. And nothing prevents others from starting a new natural estate for Newton to compete with the mismanaged estate.

Volitional science recognizes that more than one person can independently come up with the same innovation. For example, Newton and Leibniz each invented the calculus independently. Such things are easily handled by the compensation system I will describe shortly.

You may think the obligation to pay Newton and other innovators royalties for using their ideas would result in higher prices for everything. You may think the bookkeeping and accounting would be interminably difficult. But you would be wrong. The results would be an acceleration in innovation, far higher-quality products and services, and far lower prices.

Innovation is the ultimate source of higher-quality products at ever-lower prices. The first computers were huge machines costing millions of dollars. Sixty years of relentless innovation driven by entrepreneurs such as Thomas Watson, Bill Gates, and Steve Jobs have delivered far more powerful computers that cost far less and that we carry around in our pockets. As for the difficulty of accounting for such royalties, today's accountants spend most of their time navigating the insanely complex details of tax returns. They are calculating to an insane level of detail how much the state will steal from you. Tomorrow's accountants will have a far nobler mission: helping entrepreneurs keep track of royalties owed to innovators, thus, at long last, producing market justice for those whose work underpins the growth of civilization.

Question: If markets tend to compensate individuals based on the value they create for others, why have they left out the one class of individuals who create the most value for others—scientific innovators?

Answer: Scientific innovators have been kept out of the market by the custom of public domain. Since scientists began creating explanations of natural phenomena, it has been assumed such explanations should be free and open to everyone, including Hitler, Mao, Vladimir Putin, the Ayatollahs who run Iran, and whomever the American president may be. Such political leaders have applied physical science to build weapons of mass destruction. That is something we can no longer afford if we want to survive and ultimately prosper.

The theory of primary property in volitional science demonstrates how to create market justice for scientific innovators. Once this theory is implemented, they will be paid as a direct function of the value they produce. Their proper compensation will be an expression of gratitude, the market acknowledgment for value received.

The Product Development Process

Let's step back to view the situation from a larger perspective. Economists and social theorists have overlooked that production doesn't begin when entrepreneurs build factories, design equipment, or tool up machines and assembly lines. Production begins with individuals who think, and they should be compensated accordingly, as outlined in this formula:

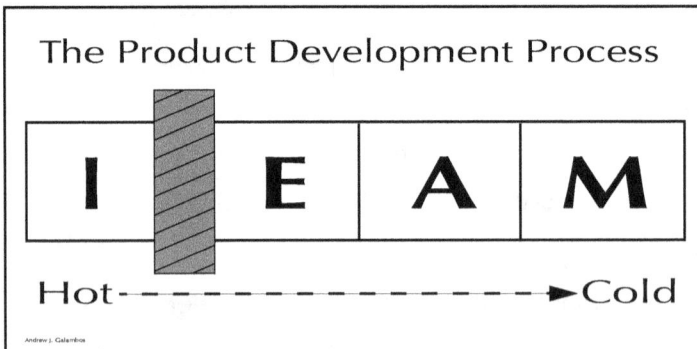

The Product Development Process

| I | E | A | M |

Hot - - - - - - - - - - - - ► Cold

Andrew J. Galambos

This formula depicts the Product Development Process (PDP), formerly called the Ideological Program. Creative thinking, labeled **I** for innovation, is the beginning of production called the *Hot End*. All products begin in the Hot End. The gray bar represents the disclosure barrier between innovators and everyone else, especially entrepreneurs. In today's world, that barrier prevents the proper treatment of major innovators. The process flows from the Hot End into the second step, called **E**, for education or entrepreneurship. Innovation is transmitted to entrepreneurs, engineers, and technicians who use their creative imagination to use the new ideas to develop better products and services.

The third step is labeled **A** for advertising, which includes marketing and distribution. This is where marketers introduce the new products to potential customers, and it is also where distribution occurs. The fourth step is labeled **M** for maintenance because when consumers buy products, they create the return revenue flowing back upstream, sustaining production at each step.

The **PDP formula** captures the entire spectrum of productive activity. Standard economics leaves out innovation and focuses on production, distribution, and consumption, with an emphasis on consumption. It advocates legal constraints on producers per Marx's slogan, "Production for use, not for profit." Few economists understand that profit measures how effectively entrepreneurs serve others. With the exception of the Austrian School, most current economics is a dismal pseudoscience. Even the Austrian School ignores innovation, the true origin of the production cycle that lies behind the disclosure barrier—the gray bar between steps one and two. The bar represents the barrier keeping innovators out of the market and opening them up to theft, as well as mental and physical attacks. Consider the murder of Giordano Bruno, the willful theft of Wilbur Wright's innovations that drove him to an early death, and the tragic mistreatment of Nikola Tesla.

Scientists who develop major new ideas tend to be ignored, resented, and harassed in that order. But if their ideas are better than previous explanations, the new ideas will survive. Their innovations will filter through the disclosure barrier only to be stolen or adapted by others who will use them to produce and market goods and services from which they, not the innovators, reap the financial and other benefits. Only then does the standard economic concept of production begin.

Very few people spend their lives in the first step. Most people don't even know it exists. When they discover that innovators exist, they view them as eccentric weirdos who rock the boat with crazy ideas. But innovators are the ultimate source of production and progress. The first and second steps together make up production. But the first step comes before the second, both chronologically and logically. Creative thinking produces the ideas, goals, and plans from which all production flows. Innovative thinking is required to bring a product into being that's never previously existed.

Before conceiving a product, one must consider more abstract ideas: How is the universe structured? What causes things to happen? What constitutes a good explanation of natural phenomena? The answers are called scientific laws and theories. To create sustainable progress, someone must discover and apply the laws of nature that explain how the universe works. We cannot yet control and change the universe's fundamental structure; we can only study it and develop explanations of how it works. From those theoretical explanations of natural phenomena, we develop technological applications.

This brings us to the second step, **E**, for education and entrepreneurship. It includes design, manufacturing, and all aspects of production. Educability and production are linked because only educable people are capable of high production. To achieve a durable spacefaring civilization, we must create a natural proprietary channel between the first and second steps in place of the disclosure barrier. When this happens, innovators and entrepreneurs will seek to cooperate, unleashing a production system of unprecedented power.

Steps one and two are forms of production. The first step, innovation, is the more important phase. Step two involves the less important but creatively necessary phase of entrepreneurial production. Everything else will flow smoothly when those steps are linked cooperatively instead of antagonistically. We won't have to worry about how goods are distributed. That part of the process will take care of itself once a proper production system is established.

The PDP formula is neither political nor anti-political. It has little to do with distribution and consumption, the part of the process on which economic bureaucrats focus. They believe they can help consumers by interfering with producers and distributors through coercive regulations. The only help producers need, however, is a social system of secure property rights that leaves them alone. Whenever bureaucrats interfere in production, they obstruct and diminish the source of all goods and services. By inhibiting production, bureaucrats produce impoverishment.

Timescales

The key to survival and prosperity is integrating the first two steps, innovation and production, in a long-term, mutually profitable relationship. That's easier said than done. Innovators and entrepreneurs have different objectives. Entrepreneurs are in business for a profit. If they don't make a profit, they've got a problem. They must satisfy their investors. They must satisfy fickle customers. They must regularly pay associates and vendors.

To prosper, we need entrepreneurs willing to think in far longer timeframes than the next quarter, year, or decade. In the six thousand years of recorded history, major cultures have risen and fallen. To avoid this fate, we need a new kind of entrepreneur and business structure. Such entrepreneurs must be different from today's business executives. They must have a very different intellectual orientation. They must recognize the significance of something few business or intellectual leaders understand: the four timescales in which human achievement occurs—*trivial, personal, species,* and *cosmic.*

Today's businesses exist mainly in the *trivial* timescale. A few outstanding executives think a generation or two ahead using the *personal* timescale. Entrepreneurs and innovators of the future will have to move up to the *species* timescale. Major innovators and a small number of entrepreneurs are, for the most part, not motivated by a desire for recognition and fame during their lifetime. Historically, they've gotten little or no satisfaction from how contemporaries responded to their work. They think in the *species* timescale.

The most important innovators are scientists who discover better explanations about the physical universe or one of its domains. A scientist is not someone with a degree from a major university but anyone who develops a better or more useful explanation of natural phenomena than existing ones. For instance, Wilbur Wright, who never attended a college or university, is a major scientist. Such individuals view themselves and their work in the context of the *species* timescale. Their accomplishments did not occur in a vacuum. They always build on earlier ideas, sometimes discovered thousands of years prior. As Newton said, "If I have seen farther than others, it is because I am standing on the shoulders of giants." Scientific innovators build on past ideas to create new knowledge their successors will use ad infinitum.

Anchor Point of History (APH)

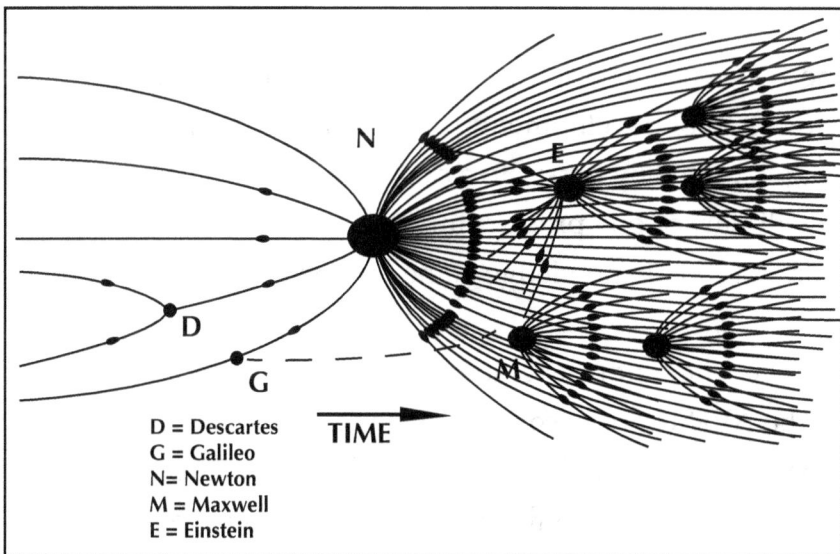

D = Descartes
G = Galileo
N= Newton
M = Maxwell
E = Einstein

TIME

Galambos created the APH chart above. It is related to the PDP formula. The chart depicts the historical flow of ideas involved in a *product* and those that flow out from it into the future, while the PDP formula represents the *process* by which products are created. Both have an arrow representing a directional flow. In the APH chart, the arrow is time. In the PDP formula, the arrow symbolizes the production flow from its source to its goal: distribution and consumption. It represents both time and the development process.

The APH chart is the total market—past, present, and future. Past knowledge feeds into and drives everything being developed in the present, which, in turn, becomes the pressure that feeds into the future. Production flows from genesis to fulfillment. When we think about the process, we realize specific products come and go, but the product lines can continue indefinitely.

In free market capitalism, as products become obsolete, new knowledge is mined from their developmental history to produce more advanced derivative products. We don't use the two-wheel chariots of the Roman Empire, but there is a direct line of development from the chariot to the four-wheel wagon pulled by horses to a car propelled by an engine. They are all part of one product line. We use the cumulative, constantly refined knowledge gained in the past to create today's products.

The integrator-developer of a product, the central point of the APH chart, becomes the market for those who created past achievements. He is using their work. Those past innovators, in turn, were the market for previous generations of products, including knowledge developed by earlier individuals. Prior knowledge fulfills itself in later markets. When we extend that indefinitely, we enter the *species* timescale.

For trivial products, the timescale may be very short. But for a scientific theory indispensable for such an important venture as space exploration, we're dealing with the *cosmic* timescale. If we transcend political barbarism and expand into the cosmos, the *species* timescale will grow into the *cosmic* timescale, and we will grow with it.

The **N** at the center of the APH chart stands for Newton. He is central because all previous knowledge fed into Newton, who integrated it into explanations that became the basis of all scientific progress thereafter. Newton is the Anchor Point of History. Full stop. No one else will ever occupy this position.[2] However, we can also generalize the process into a universal concept. In that case, the **N** can represent any product or achievement, whether trivial or important.

The chart depicts the genesis and development of products in general over time. Every product has input ideas from the past. Someone originally conceived those input ideas. The letters **G**, **D**, **N**, **M**, and **E** represent Galileo, Descartes, Newton, Maxwell, and Einstein in the original chart of humanity's historical development. We can replace those letters with symbols representing other individuals, products, or ideas. **N** could represent the integrator-developers of any product. They could be entrepreneurs or innovators who assimilate the input components into successful new products such as computers, iPhones, or rocket ships. A computer is created from a variety of component ideas from different streams of knowledge that the developer integrates into a marketable product. There will also be a market flowing horizontally from those products into future products.

New products will lead to more advanced products in an unrestricted process of cultural evolution. These include first-generation improvements as well as second-, third-, and tenth-generation derivatives of the product. Some of these iterations will be distinctly different from the original but were suggested by it. Current products become the catalyst for developing later products, whether five years or five centuries later.

The integrator-developer draws upon past innovation. In the chart, time flows from left (the past) to right (the future) through the center (the present), which is the integration point of any product. The farther upstream on the chart, the more remote we are in the past. The inputs from the left represent ideas entrepreneurs and technical developers apply that have flowed through time to the present. The lines flowing out to the right from the integration point represent the future. The future is downstream, and the past is upstream from where we stand. The important point is the continuity in these flows. That continuity is the Portrait of Civilization.

Portrait of Civilization
The continuity of civilization results from the flow of ideas that do not perish, created by individuals who do. Discontinuity in civilization results from the chaos produced by political coercion. The past drives the future. If we have a prosperous, durable civilization, it is because we learned from the

past. If we have a disintegrating civilization, it means we let prior knowledge decay. We currently have a mix of the two. We've forgotten how to distinguish between what's valuable and what's not.

The things from the past worth preserving are innovations and the knowledge flowing from them. We must also learn from the past to reject coercion, particularly political coercion. Yet almost every history class in almost every school celebrates coercion. The great heroes are kings, presidents, generals, soldiers, rabble-rousers, and political leaders. The key events are wars, battles, rebellions, political movements, and legislation. If someone mentions the French Revolution, most do not think of d'Alembert, Lavoisier, Laplace, Lagrange, Voltaire, or Paine but of the despicable little tyrants Robespierre, Marat, and Danton. A more accurate history would tell the story of those whose work created and built civilizations. It would focus on innovators and entrepreneurs, not kings and generals.

Mises's branch of Austrian Economics[3] developed a method of reasoning that led to brilliant new explanations of social phenomena. Volitional science integrates Mises's epistemology with physics, the source of our most valuable knowledge of the universe. The APH chart depicts the evolutionary market giving rise to a method of studying natural phenomena that continuously generates more useful explanations and ruthlessly eliminates erroneous ones.

When we apply scientific knowledge to build something, it works. When we apply scientific engineering to build a bridge, it will stand. The Brooklyn Bridge is still handling traffic after 150 years. When we apply science to build cars and roads, we can drive wherever the roads take us. With science, we can travel to the moon and beyond. We will develop scientific knowledge of living systems that will allow us to cure cancer, reverse aging, and extend the youthful portion of our lifespan for millennia. Space exploration and biomedical progress are the new frontiers of science.

In a system of free cultural evolution, every input creates more output. Free market evolution is a highly efficient system that gives rise to order rather than disorder. It accords with the directional flow of life. Life evolves in the direction of greater order and lesser disorder. By continually developing outputs of greater value, we will gain the ideological leverage to drive the expansion of civilization. That's why the APH chart is the Portrait of Civilization.

Simple Answers

When it comes to fair compensation for scientific innovations, volitional science poses three important questions and answers them:

1. **Why we pay** anyone is gratitude, the market acknowledgment, where due, for value received.
2. **Who we pay** are those from whom we've received value, including those responsible for the historical development of their products and the knowledge necessary to create them.
3. **How much we pay** is determined by each entrepreneur's or user's assessment of the relative value each

individual's work contributed to the revenue flow a product generates.

These components are all that is necessary to create a proper system of compensation. Their intelligent application will produce justice. When someone creates value for us, we compensate them accordingly. When someone harms us, they compensate us for the damage. The latter is restitution or "negative squared compensation." When proper compensation becomes the customary way of paying people, there will be little need for restitution.

These ideas are more radical than you may suspect. When explained carefully over time, however, they will seem common sense. Volitional science encompasses frames of reference vastly larger in time and creative potential than any previous concept of society. It takes time to grasp its implications and entailments, but the fundamental theory is very simple.

★ ★ ★

Recap

- Any system for compensating scientific innovators based on universal principles must address two problems: (1) how to fairly compensate those who are dead and (2) how to create noncoercive systems to register, protect, disseminate, and compensate those who create intellectual property going forward. Volitional science addresses both issues.

- Private registration companies could be set up to verify ownership of intellectual property and publish public databases of ideas entrepreneurs could use under two conditions: (1) no coercive use and (2) payment of a non-zero royalty.

- A natural estate is a perpetual financial entity set up to register ownership and receive compensation for an individual's work. Initially, many entities would compete to represent major innovators, but the free market would naturally winnow competitors to very few and, eventually, but not necessarily, just one.

- The Product Development Process (PDP) captures the entire spectrum of production as it flows from innovation through the barrier between innovation and the entrepreneurs who use the new ideas to develop better products and services.

- The Anchor Point of History (APH) chart depicts the total market—past, present, and future. Past knowledge feeds into everything being currently developed, which feeds into the future. The **N** at the center of the chart stands for Isaac Newton because all previous knowledge flows to us through him. The **N** could also represent integrator-developers of any product.

- The continuity of civilization results from the flow of ideas that do not perish, created by people who do. The past drives the future. If we have a prosperous civilization, it is because we learned from the past. If we have a disintegrating civilization, it means we let prior knowledge decay. We currently have a mix of the two.

- There are three important questions regarding proper compensation for scientific innovation, to which volitional science gives the following answers:

  1. Why we pay anyone is gratitude, the market acknowledgment, where due, for value received.
  2. Who we pay are those from whom we've received value, including those responsible for the historical development of their products and the knowledge necessary to create them.
  3. How much we pay is determined by each entrepreneur's or user's assessment of the relative value each individual's work contributed to the revenue flow a product generates.

8

Exchange Equivalences and Property

The progressive development of man is vitally dependent on invention. It is the most important product of his creative brain. Its ultimate purpose is the complete mastery of mind over the material world, the harnessing of the forces of nature to human needs. This is the difficult task of the inventor who is often misunderstood and unrewarded.

—Nikola Tesla

THE CONCEPT OF PROPERTY at the heart of volitional science will affect how we think about knowledge and the pioneers who discover it. It will change everything about our lives by leading to new corporate structures, financial systems, investment mechanisms, compensation methods, and far more effective money and credit systems. It will support a potentially infinite increase of knowledge, which means we will always pursue fascinating challenges even after we've become unimaginably wealthy in a Spaceland civilization. We will always be near the beginning of infinity.

One of the problems in understanding how to handle property is that, until now, no one has figured out how to make proprietary exchange equivalences among the three kinds of property—primordial, primary, and secondary. That's why money, a form of secondary property, has never effectively reflected and protected the value of people's achievements. The dependence on secondary property as the basis of economic value in political cultures is why no social structure has ever been permanent. To most people, the only valid concept of property *is* secondary (tangible) property. They don't see a correlation between the value of life itself and the ideas that make life worth living. Today's stock market implicitly recognizes ideas by the huge value investors place on the most innovative high-tech companies. However, it is only implicit and not connected directly to the ownership of IP.

An Analogy

Galambos began his explanation of exchange equivalences this way: The lack of exchange equivalences among the three kinds of property is analogous to the evolutionary understanding of energy in nineteenth-century physics. Before then, the concept of energy was poorly understood. Newton's three laws of motion and his accompanying explanation in the *Principia Mathematica* provided the first modern understanding of energy. He recognized that kinetic and potential energy were two different kinds of energy continually seesawing back and forth.

Newton was the first to realize that energy exhibits more than one form and possesses a conservation factor, meaning the total amount of energy doesn't change as it takes different forms. His work triggered a surge of new knowledge about the physical world, which led to our modern concept of energy. By the middle of the nineteenth century, Mayer and Joule had discovered the first law of thermodynamics, which describes the equivalence of heat and mechanical energy and confirms that the total amount of energy remains the same as energy changes from one form into another. Still later in the nineteenth century, the principle was generalized to electrical, magnetic, and all other forms of energy, including the internal kinetic energy of molecules. All these manifestations of energy were integrated into a single concept.

In the first decade of the twentieth century, Einstein showed that mass is a form of energy ($e=mc^2$). His discovery is the most recent integration in the evolution of the conservation of energy principle. As physics has evolved, its discoveries in various fields have been integrated through a single concept: the conservation of energy.

Developing our understanding of the equivalences among the different forms of energy led to enormous progress in physics. It allows us to explain more and more things through energy. In one sense, all physics is a study of transformations from one kind of energy to another. But that's only useful if you can measure the equivalences. This entails knowing the equivalence factors among, for example, electrical, chemical, and mechanical energy, consisting of kinetic energy, potential energy, and mass.

If you don't understand those correlations, don't know how to translate from one to another, or don't know the methods for determining their equivalences, you can't understand the processes of nature. Understanding those equivalences makes physics intelligible. We can measure the coherence of our understanding of nature by how successfully we deal with those energy equivalences. Likewise, the proper handling of proprietary equivalences will lead to a volitional technology that is understandable and workable. That's the direct connection.

NETCOs

When we have a mechanism that is adaptable to both scientific and economic concerns and integrates primary property (P1) with secondary property (P2), this will create proper monetary exchange equivalences between the various forms of property. Only then will we be able to put a price on primary achievements and attract funding for innovation on a grand scale. We will have a market mechanism that can estimate the present value of an idea in monetary terms. However, it is important to understand that value is only realized over time as entrepreneurs apply an idea to the creation of products and services that are offered in the market. Thus, compensation is anchored in reality and emerges from real market transactions that generate revenue.

In chapter 7, I explained the concept of a natural estate. Each person's natural estate begins at birth and lasts forever. It is the cumulative store and record of their accomplishments throughout their lives. The formation of natural estates would give rise to another market entity, the NETCO, a Natural Estate Trust Company.

NETCO (Natural Estate Trust Company): A company that manages the estates of people during and after their lifetimes. It will develop market systems to identify the value of innovations in the early stages, which would allow market specialists (or anyone for that matter) to place a speculative bet on new ideas before they're applied on a large scale.

Such entities would be particularly important for managing the natural estates of inventors and innovators. The capital accumulating in these NETCOs would be an ideal source of funds to invest in further innovations, including audacious projects more conservative fund managers wouldn't touch. Examples might include funding the development of major fundamental advances in biological science leading to unlimited youthful lifespans. They could also fund research into the physical science and technology to design rocketry to transport humans to Mars and build the habitats to live there. From there, the next stop could be to travel beyond the solar system to the Andromeda galaxy, our nearest celestial neighbor. A NETCO has a natural incentive to grow its P2 by propagating its owners' ideas. And who better to fund space exploration than Newton's natural estate? He could certainly afford it.

A NETCO is one of the entities that will work closely with companies that register ownership, monitor usage, and track payment for inventions and innovations. They will develop market systems to identify value in its early stages and place a speculative bet on innovations before they're applied on a large scale. It's a more refined approach to funding innovation and a natural evolutionary step from today's venture capital market. The valuation process could develop into a major form of speculation—a futures market in new ideas and theories driven by highly qualified professional speculators. Investment and speculation are two different things. Speculation takes more talent and knowledge than investing. Speculation is a necessary function in a high-level culture. There's nothing immoral about it.

A professional class will emerge with the skills to speculate on the potential value of current innovations. They will develop proprietary ways to evaluate the significance of new knowledge before it produces revenue from market applications. Anyone with an interest in this field could participate. Based on that information, innovators or their NETCOs could sell shares representing a percentage of future royalties for a specified time in exchange for an up-front payment, which would provide the innovator or NETCO with immediate money the innovator could use to buy a house or car or to reinvest in new innovations. The amount would represent the present value of estimated payments that would flow in over years, decades, or centuries. Futures markets will emerge in which people participate in the revenue shares and royalties to be earned by innovators in exchange for a stipulated sum of money. It could be an auction market—bid and ask.

An innovator's agent or NETCO could auction off 10 percent of the royalties on a new idea for one hundred years.

Ten percent for two hundred or four hundred years would be worth more; 10 percent of the royalties forever would command a much larger price. These transactions would be managed by speculators who evaluate each one on an at-risk basis. If they evaluate correctly, they'll make money in the present, while NETCOs (and their managers) will make more money overall. If they get it wrong, speculators will lose money, and a NETCO will make less than it would have. That's why NETCO trustees must have a *species* timescale attitude. Without it, they would not know how to evaluate innovation in the long run.

New Markets

Entrepreneurs will normally pay for innovation via a royalty on the revenue it generates in the market over time. No one receives a royalty until the innovation produces revenue. That's a very different mechanism than donating to innovators, which wealthy people now do before any results are produced. In contrast, a royalty (revenue share) is paid only after the entrepreneur paying the royalty has produced revenue from its applications. Compensation is tethered to real results, not some pie-in-the-sky promise of eventual returns, as in multilevel marketing schemes. This will become the normal way of paying innovators, but it produces a timescale problem.

A major innovator may not receive royalties for years, decades, or centuries, depending on the revolutionary nature of the breakthrough. Aristarchus, a Greek who developed a heliocentric model of the solar system some 1,800 years before

Copernicus, had to wait two thousand years for recognition. He would have had to wait longer for royalties. And posthumous royalties would not give him funds to pay for his groceries or invest in more research. Royalties work well but often take a long time to come in. That's why there will be revenue share speculation on discounted values.

Technological innovators could put revenue shares for specific ideas on the market with an offer to assign a percentage of the royalties to "Jones" for "X" years in exchange for "Y" dollars now. This type of offer would not affect the innovator's other royalties, just the royalty on that one product. It would be a separate transaction, exclusive of other innovations.

Getting buyers and sellers to agree will be awkward at first because there's no experience with this sort of transaction. But things would soon settle down. Markets engender an efficient process of price discovery, which is an essential information-generating system only occurring in markets.

As new markets evolve, people will get more comfortable with these kinds of transactions, and their estimates will improve with experience. The criterion for success is mutual profit between innovators and entrepreneurs. The futures market in innovation will evolve into what will be considered a normal market. It's one of many new kinds of markets that will emerge. Royalties—in this case, revenue shares on primary property—will increase to amounts unimaginable today.

It's important to understand that an entrepreneur will choose a set amount to pay for innovation royalties, say 10 percent of gross company revenue. He will take 100 percent of that amount and divide it as royalties according to his estimation of the importance of an innovator's ideas to the product line and how close in time the innovator is to the entrepreneur's current ventures. He must never violate the 10 percent allocation. That's what keeps him in reality. It is important to keep in mind in these discussions that we are talking about royalties paid in a civilization with no state; thus, entrepreneurs would pay no taxes nor face bureaucratic regulations.

The price of an innovation will become a function of the value it produces in perpetuity. If an innovator were to license his novel ideas or inventions in exchange for a one-off lump sum payment, he would not come out well in the long run. That would be an irrational contract. Innovation should generate revenue for as long as it delivers value. It can be commuted in advance in the futures markets described above. But remember, you cannot transfer or sell the ownership of primary property; you can only license it for specific or general usage or sell a share of the money it earns. That's an important distinction. However, the owner is free to sell some of the potential financial benefits of his work for a lump sum now. That's a reasonable market transaction, which allows innovators to get paid in the short run.

NRD and ARD

Galambos suggested two ways to license new ideas or inventions, which he called **Negotiated Remoteness Dilution (NRD)** and **Automatic Remoteness Dilution (ARD)**. Let's focus on the first term of each phrase, the N and the A.

Initially, when innovators (or their NETCOs) disclose innovations, they would negotiate a royalty with entrepreneurs who want to use their ideas. All long-term royalties must dilute over time for reasons I will explain shortly. But, innovators tend to dislike the nitty-gritty of such commercial negotiations. For the most part, their scientific brilliance does not extend to business dealings. They'd rather spend their time thinking, experimenting, and coming up with new ideas. But in the early stages of the evolution into a spacefaring civilization, before primary markets have matured into a smoothly operating network of profit-seeking companies, and while everyone is adjusting to this evolving system, innovators will have to negotiate the terms of access and usage. Most of them will use agents or NETCOs to negotiate on their behalf. Innovators will be free to negotiate licenses even in mature primary markets, but once ARD has been established, innovators will use it rather than NRD to license their work.

ARD is a revolutionary concept to address many objections regarding the practical logistics of owning and licensing ideas. When an idea is released via Automatic Remoteness Dilution, there is no negotiation. Something different occurs. The idea or invention is released openly to the market according to the two terms: (1) no coercive usage and (2) payment of a non-zero royalty. The buyers, at their sole discretion, determine how they will apply it and how much they will pay. This methodology represents a theoretical revolution in economics. It applies to scientific ideas or any products that can be released to the market.

ARD will quickly become the standard method of releasing and licensing ideas. Here's what that means. Today, the seller sets the price of a product. The buyer says yes or no. What's revolutionary in the new approach is that to make it automatic, the owner, who is the seller, says, "As long as you fulfill the two terms of the license—noncoercive usage and a positive non-zero royalty—the innovation is open for anyone to use."

When an innovator releases something under these two restrictions, he's saying: "I own this property. I'm making it available to everyone so long as they don't use it coercively and are willing to pay me something more than zero. They have my permission to use my idea and to determine the price they'll pay. Go for it!" That's what an ARD release means.

If you think this opens the innovator up to abuse, you'd be mistaken. It would be so in Flatland, but in Spaceland, ARD comes integrated with many other things. Alvin Lowi, Jr. suggested the use of those terms as shorthand for today's world (Flatland) and the free civilization of the future proposed by volitional science (Spaceland). Both terms come from Edwin Abbott's wonderful little book *Flatland: A Romance of Many Dimensions.*[1] Its protagonist is a two-dimensional square living in a flat, two-dimensional world who one day discovers the world of three dimensions and is astonished at its wonders. When he returns to his flat world and describes what he has seen, no one believes him. The poor square is branded a criminal and jailed for heretical views.

In the market system that develops from volitional science, this methodology for compensating innovators and releasing their ideas to the market will produce no long-term catastrophes. There may be a few short-term dislocations at first. Market evolution is never problem-free, but markets adapt quickly and positively to change. What's revolutionary with ARD is the buyer has the seller's permission to set the price he pays as long as he honors the two contractual terms.

When someone transfers authority to set the price to a buyer, it eliminates the need to negotiate. Besides the distinction between negotiating or not negotiating when licensing an idea, ARD and NRD differ in only one other way—how they structure the introduction of a product (innovation) to the market. Entrepreneurs and their accountants would calculate compensation similarly in both cases. Revenue share compensation would be governed by remoteness dilution, the R and D in NRD and ARD.

If the buyer decides on a price he later wants to change in this novel payment structure, he will do so via a simple process involving a multiplicative factor. To adjust the price, he would multiply it by a number greater than or less than one. If it's greater than one, he increases the payment; if it's less than one, he decreases it. He adjusts the payments through a simple algorithmic process. I'll cover the specifics a bit later.

The more universal the innovation, the more feasible it is to release it to ARD as soon as possible. One would release a law of nature, e.g., Newton's law of gravitation or Einstein's e=mc², to ARD much sooner than a new kind of mousetrap, which would be too trivial to release to ARD. Its value has a short market life.

Open-End Concept

The remoteness dilution mechanism depends on the **open-end concept**. There is a parallel concept in mathematics that works well for compensating innovators: the convergent infinite series.

$$1/2 + 1/4 + 1/8 + 1/16 + \ldots 1/1024 + \ldots$$
$$1/2, 3/4, 7/8, 15/16 \ldots 1023/1024 \ldots$$

In the first of these two series of fractions, all the numerators are one. Each denominator is twice as large as the previous one. We get something interesting when we add these fractions serially—the second series. The first term in the first series adds up to one-half. The first and second terms ($1/2 + 1/4$) add up to three-quarters. The first, second, and third terms add up to seven-eighths. The first, second, third, and fourth terms add to fifteen-sixteenths. Do you see what's happening in the second series? The next term in the series is always equal to a fraction in which the denominator is the next power of two, and the numerator is the denominator less one. The tenth term in the series of sums is $1023/1024$. The tenth term in the original series is one over two to the 10th power ($1/2^{10}$), which is $1/1024$.

The sum of the first ten terms in the original series will be 1023 divided by 1024. We're getting closer and closer to one. As you go to an infinite number of terms, the series will never go beyond one but approach it in the asymptote (a line continually approaching a given curve but never meeting it). Even with an infinite number of terms, it never blows up but converges on a finite sum. All long-term royalties must make use of a convergent series. Even if you were to have an infinite number of terms, it would still add up to a finite sum. That's how volitional science accounts for financial value in a booming long-term market.

Each generation of royalty payments will correspond to one term in the convergent series. You don't have to use this particular series; you can use others. The only thing necessary is that it converges. Entrepreneurs will choose series that fit the economic realities of their specific operation. The convergent series above is a reasonable default. It could become the standard to compute innovators' royalties for the entire compensation mechanism.

An entrepreneur has to be realistic. That means first-generation innovators closest to the enterprise in time will get the largest portion of the revenue share. The first generation is paid directly. Second-generation innovators upstream from first-generation innovators would get a smaller percentage share of the royalty. Third-generation innovators would get the next smaller percentage share, and so on. This wouldn't work as compensation for shorter-term associates or temporary laborers, but for innovation, it works beautifully.

Let's apply the convergent infinite series to NRD and ARD. The first generation is the person or persons immediately responsible for conceiving and developing the product. These could be inventors, innovators, designers, engineers, or those who discovered the scientific concepts that were directly applied to create and manufacture the product. For example, William Shockley used a revolutionary breakthrough in solid-state physics to develop the theoretical basis of arguably the most significant invention of the twentieth century—the transistor. He and his extraordinary assistants—technical chemist Walter Brattain and an expert in quantum theory, John Bardeen—would be the first generation to receive royalties for the transistor.

The innovators who developed quantum theory, such as Max Planck, Ernest Rutherford, Niels Bohr, Albert Einstein, Werner Heisenberg, Erwin Schrödinger, and maybe Linus Pauling, would be the second generation. The third generation would include James Clerk Maxwell, Henri Poincaré, James Jeans, John Willam Strutt, J. J. Thomson, Ludwig Boltzmann, and many others. These are ideological, not biological, generations. They are historical idea connections. One person's ideas influence someone else's ideas, which influence someone else's, and so on.

The payment fraction to these generations corresponds to the term of the convergent series. If we use the convergent series above, the payment fraction of the royalty would be 1/2 for the first generation, 1/4 for the second, 1/8 for the third, 1/16 for the fourth, and so on. The entrepreneur allocates half of the total royalties to the first generation, a quarter to the second generation, an eighth to the third, and so on. And despite what could be a large series of generations, it never blows up because it uses a convergent series. That's a key to the workability of this system.

An entrepreneur could choose a fixed percentage of revenue, say 5 percent, to pay innovators. All innovator royalties must fit within that 5 percent. The mathematics allows an entrepreneur to easily adjust the percentage to accord with the criterion of optimizing profits over the long term. Still, total royalties paid to innovators must remain within a fixed percentage or it would quickly get out of hand.

Calculating Royalties

For the sake of simplicity, let's use a trivial invention, a spring-lever mousetrap, to illustrate how ARD works. The trap has a board with a spring, and you put cheese on a little lever. When a mouse touches the cheese, it releases the spring, which brings down the levered clamp to break the poor mouse's back. The design has been around for a long time. Let's call the inventor Mr. X. Many different ideas have gone into his invention. I'll name just two: Archimedes' principle of the lever and Robert Hooke's principle of the spring. Mr. X combined those ideas with other ideas to invent the mousetrap.

How would we weigh the value of those three inputs: Archimedes, Hooke, and Mr. X? Let's say Archimedes and Hooke each get 10 percent of total royalties—not 10 percent of sales. Mr. X gets 80 percent. A smaller percentage goes to Archimedes and Hooke, and the largest share goes to Mr. X. This doesn't mean Mr. X's invention is more important than Archimedes' principle of the lever or Hooke's theories of the spring and elastic motion. Those are universal concepts from the background of knowledge human beings have developed and accumulated that Mr. X drew on to invent his device.

The entrepreneur who manufactures and sells the mousetrap receives all the income from making and marketing the trap. That's his compensation. He pays Mr. X 100 percent of the royalty, of which Mr. X assigns certain percentages to those from whom he got his basic knowledge. If Archimedes and Hooke each get 10 percent, it means Mr. X considered their ideas a valuable input to the invention. Do you see what this achieves? It's a very high-level justice mechanism. Proper compensation is positive justice.

The greatest innovators are those who attract the most accounts. Their share of any royalty will be highly diluted. The universal range of applications derived from their ideas will allow them to make it up on volume. Very few technological goods sold today would not owe a royalty to Archimedes. But equally crucial is that Archimedes had nothing to do with inventing the mousetrap or other current technical products in which his ideas are used. He created knowledge long ago that the inventors of those products used.

Say you have an idea or invention you want to license. An entrepreneur offers to pay $1 per unit of the product derived from your idea for twenty years. You have a rough idea of what you will get based on projections of how many units the entrepreneur will sell. The alternative would be to release your idea to the world via ARD and give all entrepreneurs access. If your idea is trivial and sales of the products in which it is used will swiftly fade, take the short-term payment. If you have created something you believe is important and will multiply in value over time, the non-zero positive ARD will produce far higher returns, no matter how good the short-term offer seems.

George Westinghouse offered Nikola Tesla a royalty of $1 per horsepower that Tesla's concept of an alternating current electrical system delivered over time, plus a million dollars in advance in exchange for the exclusive right to develop and build out AC distribution. Although it would have made Tesla a lot of money, it would not have been as good as an ARD royalty. Author John J. O'Neill estimated Tesla lost $12 million (c. $450 million in today's dollars) when Westinghouse's financial backers, over his objections, canceled the royalty contract. Tesla got the $1 million, but he never got the royalties. Westinghouse's chintzy financial backers refused to pay them and lost out on huge future profits.

How so, you may ask.

If the bankers had paid Tesla properly and maintained an association with his creative mind, they might have become some of the richest men in the world. They would have had access to Tesla's discoveries from 1901 until he died in 1943. Instead, Tesla became a hermit and stopped disclosing his ideas. He sealed himself off from the world and disappeared behind the disclosure barrier. Westinghouse Corp. survived because they had exclusive use of Tesla's AC concept for several decades. Imagine what they might have become if they had invested in Tesla and nurtured his creative genius. Imagine what Tesla might have produced over the next forty years, given the opportunity to disclose safely and profitably!

Flexible Contracts

If an inventor were to ask for a royalty of 1 percent of gross sales of a technical invention, that would be a bad contract. One percent is too low initially and too high later. If an innovation is a good idea, it will tend to produce value for a long time. The royalty needs to be diluted as revenue increases to make funds available to pay future innovators who add value to the product line. The percentage will decrease, but for good ideas, the dollar amount will increase.

One problem with a fixed percentage is that it's inflexible, leaving no room for new accounts. That's true, no matter the percentage at which it's frozen. Any contract not allowing for remoteness dilution is a bad contract, no matter the percentage royalty. This refers to the percentage royalty paid to each innovator in the backflow stream of a major innovation and not the overall fixed percentage of revenue an entrepreneur allocates to pay for all input innovations. That overall percentage must be fixed. The entrepreneur can adjust the various percentages paid to individual innovators via a simple mathematical formula, but the overall percentage of revenue he will pay in royalties must be fixed. Flexible within, but fixed for overall royalties.

From the above, it's evident that a compensation contract must be able to evolve and adapt according to the terms of the original contract. Otherwise, it will repel new accounts and applications, which is poisonous to innovation. If the royalty is a straight percentage set in stone, one cannot add new accounts and allocate them a cut of the royalty. The alteration of a royalty cannot be arbitrary; it must be done by a pre-specified computation. In this way, the open-end concept allows for infinite future growth, meaning no limit on innovation, exploration, and expansion except the pragmatic one of entrepreneurial profitability.

★　★　★

Recap

- The concept of property affects how we think and how we live. The concept of property is to volitional science as the concept of energy is to physics. It is the idea around which volitional science is integrated.

- Each person has a natural estate that begins at birth and lasts forever. It is the cumulative store and record of his achievements throughout his life. This estate could be managed by a Natural Estate Trust Company (NETCO). A NETCO would work closely with companies that register ownership, monitor usage, and track payment for inventions and innovations.

- There are two ways to license new ideas or inventions: Negotiated Remoteness Dilution (NRD) and Automatic Remoteness Dilution (ARD).
  - When an idea is released via NRD, innovators or their NETCOs would negotiate a set royalty with entrepreneurs who want to use their ideas.
  - When an idea is released via ARD, there is no negotiation. The idea or invention is released openly to the market. Buyers determine how they will apply it and how much they will pay.

- The remoteness dilution mechanism depends on the open-end concept and convergent infinite mathematical series. All long-term royalties must use a convergent series. That's how volitional science accounts for the financial value of ideas in unrestricted markets.

- Those closest to the entrepreneurial production process are first-generation inventors, innovators, skilled technicians, designers, etc. They will get the largest portion of the revenue share. Second-generation innovators with upstream inputs into the first-generation innovators would get a smaller percentage share. Third-generation innovators would get the next smaller percentage share, and so on, per a convergent series.

- Any contract that doesn't allow for remoteness dilution is a bad contract. A contract must be able to evolve and be open to adding new innovators; otherwise, it repels new accounts and applications. But changing a royalty cannot be arbitrary; it should be done by a specified computation. The open-end concept is crucial to all the above.

9

New Business Structure

You get paid in direct proportion to the difficulty of problems you solve.

—Elon Musk

FREEDOM IS THE SOCIETAL CONDITION wherein everyone has full (100 percent) control over their property. The only way to achieve freedom is to create a proprietary structure that encourages a smooth flow of knowledge from innovator to producer and protects ownership at every step. To accomplish this, Galambos suggested a new business structure.

But first, a caveat: The market applications of volitional science described in these chapters are suggestions and educated guesses, not mandates. The open-ended entrepreneurial civilization of Spaceland can manifest through a virtually limitless number of proprietary mechanisms and business structures guided at each node in the market network by the principle of noncoercion and the standard of mutual profitability.

Keep in mind also that the business structure and compensation mechanisms were developed for Spaceland, a world with no (zero) taxes or coercive regulations. The only limiting factors on how we achieve and maintain Spaceland are the imagination, integrity, and competence of the innovators and entrepreneurs who develop the companies that support a civilization of freedom and endless stabilized growth.

Revenue Share and Equity Share

The new business structure would function with two modes of compensation: the **revenue share** and the **equity share**.

> **Revenue share:** Compensation that is a mutually negotiated percentage of gross revenue during a specified time. It is a generalization of a royalty today.

A form of revenue share that exists today is a sales commission with no salary or guaranteed minimum. It's a percentage of the revenue a salesperson generates, which percentage may vary per contractual terms. Some form of the revenue share will likely be the main form of compensation for almost everyone, including financial investors. It's the purest form of compensation in Flatland. Pay is directly correlated to value rendered.

We use gross revenue as the basis of compensation for many reasons, one of which is that it is straightforward. Calculating profit is more complex because it includes all costs incurred by a business during a specified time, such as amounts paid for supplies, land, and facilities rent, revenue share payments to investors and service providers, amortization, depreciation, and intellectual property royalties as discussed in the last chapter.

Equity share: Compensation defined as gross revenue minus all the expenses of a business during a specified time. Equity shares are the only form of compensation suitable for an entrepreneur.

The entrepreneur's equity share is gross revenue, less everything he pays out. If the result is positive, he makes a profit. If negative, he incurs a loss, in which case he has limited time to repair the deficiency. Unlike the state, he can't make up the difference by printing money or taxing his customers. He must make a profit to stay in business. Profit is the source of durability. It's the only kind of business structure that can finance its growth. A business's profit is any increase in net assets achieved through moral means.

When an entrepreneur's equity share is positive, he is operating his business competently, which means he is providing value to his customers. There have always been entrepreneurs who know how to run consistently profitable businesses. What they can learn from volitional science is how to convert their ventures into enterprises that become meaningful in the *species* timescale and generate steadily growing profits beyond anything previously imaginable.

The purpose of growing profits is not to buy mansions, yachts, or expensive German cars, although in freedom, no one will prevent that. Profits fuel a business's drive toward longer-term objectives. A successful business is a self-funding mechanism. The necessity to make a profit keeps a business grounded in reality.

Innovators and Entrepreneurs

The key to volitional science's superior concept of entrepreneurship is a new kind of relationship between innovators and entrepreneurs. In today's world, that relationship is dysfunctional due to the win-lose attitude we've inherited from socialism. Innovators see entrepreneurs getting rich off their ideas without paying them. Conversely, entrepreneurs tend to view innovators as unrealistic visionaries whose ideas are a dime a dozen. Yet they are making money from the work of innovators, living and dead, without any thought of paying them. While there are exceptions, a state of barely suppressed mutual resentment exists between these two most important classes of producers.

Entrepreneurs and business executives have little patience for people they often perceive as academic theoreticians and unrealistic dreamers. Innovators, even Albert Einstein, have reacted to businesses that exploit their work without paying them by becoming ivory tower socialists, which reinforces the mutual hostility.

The theory of compensation in volitional science shows these two classes to be natural allies. The entrepreneurs' products and profits ultimately derive from scientific innovation. That means entrepreneurs are the primary customers for innovators' ideas. Entrepreneurs turn theoretical innovation into products they sell. I use the term *product* to mean both goods and services.

A natural and mutual proprietary interest exists between these two most productive classes. Here's how we can encourage long-term relationships that will benefit them and everyone else.

In Spaceland, innovators, workers, artists, writers, accountants, salespeople, and wait staff will be paid with revenue shares. That will be the method of compensating most forms of productive activity except for the entrepreneurs' proprietary management. Everyone from Isaac Newton to janitors will be paid with a revenue share. Their compensation will be directly correlated to the value they produce for the people paying them.

Determining Value and Compensation

How do we determine value and calculate the associated compensation? In chapter 7, I disclosed the three inputs necessary to determine compensation: (1) **why**: gratitude, (2) **to whom**: those who have provided value to the payor, and (3) **how much**: the law of logarithmic stimulation (how close or far the payee is in both time to, and effect on, current production). Compensation is further governed by the entrepreneur's discretionary assessment of the value each person contributes to ongoing revenue. In each case, the ultimate criterion from the entrepreneur's perspective is what combination will maximize long-term profits.

Once an entrepreneur has made those determinations, the calculation of revenue shares is simple. I will again use the sales commission to introduce the concept. Commissions are calculated as a percentage of revenue, not profits. Salespeople have no say in decisions involving the organization and management of the company, so it would be counterproductive to pay them a percentage of the profit made on every unit sold.

Here's an example of why compensation is based on revenue rather than profits. During the first half of the twentieth century, Hollywood actors came to regret that their royalties were based on profits, which the studios manipulated by padding costs. The result was that a movie like *Gone with the Wind* could make an enormous box office but report no profits. Thus, the actors, directors, and technical people whose royalties were based on profits were paid very little. In contrast, calculating top-line revenue is simple and almost impossible to manipulate. As a result, virtually all of today's royalties and residuals (royalties paid to actors, directors, screenwriters, etc., on perpetual reruns) are based on revenue, not profits.

If an entrepreneur makes a decision that results in a loss the year a salesperson sells more products than ever, the salesperson should still be paid for the revenue he produces. If the company fails to make a profit, it's not the salesperson's fault; it's due to entrepreneurial error or a vis major (a factor beyond an entrepreneur's control).

Salespeople should be compensated as a function of their sales alone. Suppose the business makes a large profit during a year when a salesperson doesn't make many sales. Why should he get a share of increased profits? If he produced less value for the business, he should earn less. The business made a higher profit despite his efforts. Each person should be paid for the value he generates for the business. That's not only a simple concept but also an important component of justice. People should be paid according to what their efforts are worth to the one who's paying them. The entrepreneur also has to figure out what to pay everyone in the company, from janitorial staff to C-level executives, based on their contribution to company revenue.

The entrepreneur does not pay himself a revenue share for entrepreneurial services. He shoulders the risk of directing the long-term management of an enterprise. Profit is essential information he uses to guide his decisions. Without skin in the game, he cannot responsibly lead the venture forward. Everyone should be subject to an appropriate level of risk, especially the entrepreneur. Thus, his only compensation is the profits of the enterprise.

Now, an entrepreneur may provide services other than the proprietary management of the business. He may also develop new ideas and technological innovations for which he can pay himself revenue shares. If he's the source of the ideas, that's proper. In the start-up stages, he may also provide such functions as administration, bookkeeping, and marketing. If he performs such services, he would pay himself as though he were hiring someone else to provide them. If he doesn't pay for all relevant services, he isn't measuring the true profit of the business. He's also losing vital information by mixing the value of innovation, bookkeeping, and sales with the concept of profit. Profit is what's left over after paying for all services other than entrepreneurial management.

For entrepreneurial management, e.g., setting long- and short-term goals, organizing production, hiring associates, and deciding how much they're paid, the entrepreneur is compensated by an equity share alone. If he paid himself a revenue share or, worse, a salary, he'd be deluding himself. If he took an annual salary of $100K, it would come from his profit. If he didn't take the $100K, it would be additional profit.

When profit is the only compensation, the entrepreneur is taking a full proprietary risk in his management of the business. He is responsible for what products he makes and the associates he selects to produce and market them. He decides how much to pay everyone needed to deliver his products. He integrates everything necessary to create a business with the goal of increasing profits. That's the value—the effectiveness factor—for which he earns the profit.

In the new business structure of volitional science, the entrepreneur owns 100 percent of the profit. The equity share is his total and only compensation. All the profit belongs to him as the sole owner of the business. He does not share equity or profits. There are no equity stockholders. It's beyond the scope of this chapter to consider other types of business structures or partnerships, a subject I hope to take up in more detail in a subsequent book.

An entrepreneur may develop an original business structure for which he pays himself a royalty. By doing so, he isn't incurring extra costs for no reason. If he's successful, the structure will last and become more important as the business grows. At some point, he might hire others who could run the business better than he could. Their compensation would also be via the equity share the entrepreneur transfers to them. As each separate department of the business grows large enough, it would have its own entrepreneur who is responsible for the profits of that department. Thus, this structure encourages entrepreneurs to continually spin off such departments into separate businesses, with the mothership receiving a negotiated revenue share. This would free the former lead entrepreneur to start another business or pursue other things he finds more interesting. His natural estate would survive his departure as the permanent repository of his property and the residual value of his services. If others use his innovations ten years or a thousand years hence, his natural estate will earn royalties on the revenue generated.

If this sort of multiple royalty scheme seems like it would blow up, just remember that the percentage of each royalty decreases to make room for new entrants to the growing networked structure.

Buyer-Seller versus Employer-Employee

Ordinary economics assumes that most companies have an owner, called the employer, who hires workers, called employees. In volitional science, there are no employers or employees. Neither role exists in the concept of primary property. This caste system and its inherent class struggle will be dumped in the junkyard of history. Today's employees will become tomorrow's sellers of services. Today's employers will become tomorrow's buyers of services. This signals a change far deeper than mere semantics.

When people have something to sell, they make it available to others in exchange for something else, usually money. With money, people can buy things they want. But to earn that money, they must provide something of value to others. They can sell their willingness and ability to apply their knowledge and skills to someone who will pay for them. The more skilled they are, the more valuable they will be and the more money they will make.

Buyers are customers. Sellers must satisfy customers' wishes. The sellers' livelihood depends on it. Now, let's apply this principle to workers. The former employee becomes a seller; the entrepreneur becomes a buyer. The entrepreneur is a customer the worker must please, or he won't be paid for his services. This provides a powerful incentive to do a good job because an entrepreneur can always buy from someone else.

In this relationship, no smart entrepreneur would pay people according to the time they spend on the job. Compensation would be a function of how well they perform, measured by the entrepreneur's determination of how much they contribute to revenue growth. Spaceland entrepreneurs will require a far higher level of competence than Flatland managers because that's what they're paying for.

Some professionals today appear to be paid for their time, but they are actually being paid for their readiness to respond to emergencies. Police, fire personnel, doctors, and nurses who work set shifts must be on duty at certain times and days, no matter what. They are paid the same whether they are busy or not. The amount of time they spend on a task is irrelevant compared to their expertise and immediate availability. Did they save the house and the people in it? Did they prevent the crime? Did they save the patient in the ER? If they don't perform well, they don't get promoted or could lose their positions. In Spaceland, these services will be provided by private companies and contractors. If they are incompetent, entrepreneurs won't hire them.

When employees are paid for their time, there immediately exists a conflict with their employer. Their pay is not connected to success via revenue shares but to the time it takes to complete their tasks. The more lethargically they work, the more they are paid. And since their pay is unrelated to revenue, they have no incentive to consistently aim higher in their work. They are now in conflict with their employer. The more money they can extract per hour, the less the company has to reinvest in production or in hiring more productive associates. (In Spaceland, workers will be called "associates.")

This relationship has huge benefits for entrepreneurs, but it also has compensating advantages for sellers of services. They are capitalists whose capital consists of their ability to deliver, which they achieved through education and real-world experience. They are no longer employees dealing with demanding bosses. They are no longer in a master-slave relationship. They are independent suppliers in a win-win contractual relationship that encourages both parties to cooperate in pursuit of mutual profit. The sellers will have their own businesses and, thus, their own profit centers. If they want to earn and increase their pay, they must provide services that satisfy their customers (former employers). The amount they are paid will depend on the quality and quantity of their services from the buyers' point of view.

The seller of services can't afford the attitude of an employee: "Why should I make extra effort? If I put in forty hours, I get paid." Instead, he has the self-respect of knowing what he earns depends on his performance. The greater the quantity and quality of his services, the more he makes. His income depends on his ability to produce results that increase revenue and contribute to a business's long-term success.

Sellers of services have more control over their destiny. They negotiate when and under what conditions they work. They become independent contractual associates. They are neither slaves nor employees with no real stake in the business. To earn more, they will guarantee the quality of their services and pay for their mistakes. They will assume the risks and responsibilities that go with independence. They may not earn as much initially as when they were employees being paid for their time, but once they deliver results, they can make far more depending on their competence and integrity. To get started, they would be paid an advance until they begin delivering results that contribute to revenue. In Spaceland, they would pay back the advance out of future revenue share earnings.

Competitive Advantages

In Spaceland, the concept of the employee (a vassal) and their relationship to an employer (suzerain) will disappear. But since it's a noncoercive free market, people can arrange their productive relationships any way they please. If two parties agree to an employer-employee relationship with hourly wages, so be it. However, they will lose out to competitors who compensate their associates with revenue shares.

Revenue shares eliminate the inherent conflicts of the employer-employee relationship. With revenue shares, everyone in the networked enterprise works together to increase revenue, with the entrepreneur guiding the overall venture toward consistently higher profits. Such companies will far outproduce those with hourly wage employees, not only in quantity but in the quality of their products. The only constraint on a profit-seeking company is profit optimization over the long run.

In Flatland, unions can be forced on companies by legal coercion. In Spaceland, unions are not outlawed. Nothing is. A worker could attempt to set up a union inside any corporation. But when associates' pay is connected to their contribution to revenue, they will view someone forming a union to foment discord or push for higher wages unconnected to output as a pest interfering with their ability to earn more income and higher status as valued associates of an important company producing high-quality products.

Competition (and win/win cooperation) among profit-seeking companies will result in a rapid evolution of innovative company structures. Each new structure will be like a lab experiment. Does it result in higher customer satisfaction? Does it result in consistently higher profits? In free markets, the consuming public controls production by buying or not buying a company's products. As Mises noted, in a free market, the consumer is truly king. Companies must satisfy customers or go out of business.

The universe is a harsh, unforgiving place. It is constantly trying to kill us and destroy our creations. We need tough, resilient individuals producing the infrastructure and the mundane products that keep us alive and productive day in and day out. The only real protection workers need is the freedom to choose to work or not work with—not for—certain entrepreneurs or companies. They will learn to negotiate decent contractual terms for their labor. In the market competition for good contractual associates, they must constantly improve their skills or be left with less lucrative positions.

Associates can also contract with more than one company. They can become entrepreneurs in their professions, which has greater dignity and personal status than an employee-vassal. In a contractual relationship, the associate is not subordinate to the entrepreneur of even a very large corporation. They negotiate to achieve a relationship of mutual profitability. The greater the skill set an associate has developed, the more lucrative contracts he can negotiate, but ones that align with the survival and success of the entrepreneur and his company.

In Spaceland, all the incentives align, constrained at each node in the networked corporation and in the larger network of corporations by the governing principle of consistently higher profits over the long run.

Financial Investors

If entrepreneurs own 100 percent of the equity in Spaceland corporations, what do financial investors own in exchange for their capital investment? The answer is they will own revenue shares according to a specified formula. Most people will invest through open-end investment companies whose sole business is managing a portfolio of revenue shares of corporations they believe will generate steadily growing profits over the long haul. There can be as many variations on the revenue share formula as investment markets will allow. However, all will adhere to the principles and natural constraints discussed earlier.

The percentage share of revenue an investor receives must diminish over time to allow new investors to participate in the company's growth. As with revenue shares allocated to innovators, the overall percentage share of revenue going to financial investors must be fixed and remain fixed. If it is set at 10 percent, for example, that 10 percent can be divided among a theoretically infinite number of investors via the open-end concept and the use of infinite convergent series.

If you think this limits an investor's potential return, think again. Nvidia, a semiconductor company that started out designing GPUs for gaming and recently became the leader in making chips for advanced AI computation, went public in 1999 with an annual revenue of $160 million. Suppose you were an investor allocated 10 percent of the revenue shares in an investment company that bought shares worth 5 percent of annual revenue in the year Nvidia went public. Let's assume you bought those shares via the investment company for $800,000 ($160 million x .05 x 0.1). In the fiscal year ending mid-January 2024, Nvidia generated annual revenue of $60 billion. Five percent of $60 billion is $3 billion.

Let's also assume your percentage revenue share has been diluted by a factor of $1/50$, in which case you would receive an annual payment of $60 million twenty-five years later. A dilution factor of 1/10 would result in a payment of $300 million per year. That is recurring income to the investor in a civilization with no state, thus no taxes. Even when diluted by 1/50, an $800K investment has turned into an increasing, annually recurring payment of $60 million. Not a bad return. Many companies have shown Nvidia-sized returns, such as Apple, Amazon, Oracle, Visa, Berkshire Hathaway, Taiwan Semiconductor, Meta Platforms, Walmart, Alphabet (Google), and Microsoft.

Investor share allocations must be open-ended. Any time investors are willing to buy new revenue shares, the company will issue new shares ad infinitum. That means share issuance is subject to market conditions. Certain conditions detrimental to current investors may arise in the early years of the transition from Flatland to Spaceland that convinced a company to halt its issuance of new shares. The terms under which that could occur would be in the original investment contract and would usually be subject to approval by the entrepreneur or entrepreneurial group managing the company. The entrepreneur wants the best reputation possible in the investment community. He and his group want to be known as individuals who provide investors with a great long-term return. That will lead them to adjust their actions to market demands.

For start-up capital, there would be additional terms that allow a young company to retain capital in its initial years and apply it to growth. Before the company generates sufficient revenue to fund its growth, a venture investment firm might give the company five years before it pays initial revenue shares. At the same time, the investment contract might state that if the investment company owns (to make calculations simple) shares worth 10 percent of company revenue, once the company has paid back 100 percent of the original investment amount, its payment would drop from 10 percent to 9 percent and continue to drop by 1 percent for every payout of 100 percent of the initial investment until it reached say 5 percent (again for calculation purposes only) after which it would remain at 5 percent and dilute according to the open-ended grant of new shares. There are a potentially infinite number of variations on such formulas. The market would regulate by long-term profit optimization the ones that become widely applied.

The discussion above should answer most questions regarding more specialized investing categories such as angel investing, venture capital investing, later-stage venture investing, and buying shares on public markets. The revenue share contract can be tailored to fit any type of investment, from raw start-ups to seasoned growth companies. Keep in mind that in freedom, people can develop any kind of investment structure they wish. Markets are the most creative social system that has ever existed. The business structures I'm suggesting are the beginning of a long-term cultural evolution in which entrepreneurs and others create all manner of new company forms and investment architectures.

An important aspect of this approach is that it gives financial investors no control over a corporation's operation and strategic direction. Financial investors cannot "take over" a company by buying its equity shares. The entrepreneur or entrepreneurial group owns all equity shares in a corporation. Financial investors are investing in the entrepreneur or his group's ability to produce rising revenues and profits over the long run from which they will achieve their return.

There is another beautiful aspect of this structure; it makes investment crashes almost impossible. When the only type of shares available for public investing are revenue shares handled mostly through open-end investment companies, it creates an environment in which it is extremely unlikely for mass panic to occur, the kind that causes market crashes. Most investment companies would evolve into an open-ended structure. That means they would not only issue new shares according to market demand but also would guarantee to buy back shares whenever investors wanted to sell. Thus, open-end investment companies would act as a buffer to wild panics in which many people rush to sell their shares simultaneously.

Since there is no Federal Reserve or central state bank with a monopoly on issuing currency in Spaceland, there would be no attempt to spur or rein in the economy by whoever holds political power at the time. A fully free market regulates itself, ultimately guided by the naturally amalgamated profits of every company. In Spaceland, there is no state bureaucracy to manipulate the economy. Since all state interference in economic activity reduces wealth, everyone would be wealthier.

Corporations, Clearinghouses, and Bridge Corporations

Corporation: A contractual association of individuals structured to fulfill a mutually agreed proprietary purpose on a profit-seeking basis.

A corporation is a business structure that can outlive its entrepreneurial founders or its current owners. There are Flatland corporations still going strong today that have existed for hundreds of years. Kongo Gumi is a Japanese construction company reputed to be the oldest continually operating company in the world. It was founded in 578 CE and is still going strong today, albeit as a separate company within a larger construction company, Takamatsu. In Spaceland, corporations could last for thousands of years. As long as it generates profits by providing customers with value, a corporation can keep growing and thriving for millennia. That illustrates another advantage of a profit-seeking corporation: a well-run company can self-fund its growth out of profits it generates in perpetuity.

Clearinghouse: A central institution comprised of an open-ended network of an unlimited number of profit-seeking companies that collects, maintains, and distributes information about who owns what for the mutual benefit of its members.

Clearinghouses will be an emergent, integrated network of profit-seeking companies, eventually growing into millions, that will:

- Produce and maintain systems that protect primary property and facilitate primary transactions
- Administer new forms of investment and insurance
- Integrate money and credit through a competitive market process instead of through a coercive state monopoly

Clearinghouses already exist. They grew out of the need to facilitate exchanges between different banks and financial institutions. The Spaceland clearinghouse will be far larger and more important than those existing in Flatland. It will continue facilitating payments but only as one of many integrated services in a dynamic information marketplace. It will keep track of who owns what, who has transferred ownership to whom, and at what royalty rate.

All aspects of the clearinghouse are integrated through contractual agreements. It is an emergent market network comprised of thousands, eventually millions, of specialized profit-seeking ventures. Each venture is run by an entrepreneur with skin in the game. It is not a monopoly imposed by a vote of the majority or bureaucratic edict. It emerges from the market as an open-ended network of an ever-growing number of subnetworks of companies, some of which will have their own subnetworks that may have their own subnetworks, etc. Its expansion is regulated solely by the market. Each node of the network will be governed by win/win-lose/lose contracts between profit-seeking companies. Since the clearinghouse is an emergent market phenomenon, it is open-ended and thus capable of infinite expansion into the future governed only by profit, the ultimate guarantor that a business is acting morally and continues serving the public.

Its initial focus will be on accounting for primary property. When primary property owners are accurately identified and their ownership is protected, the methods developed for that purpose will automatically protect secondary (tangible) property. But if primary property is not properly protected, secondary property cannot be protected.

> **Bridge corporation:** A business structure designed to bridge the gap between the non-freedom of Flatland and the freedom of Spaceland.

One of the vehicles that will spearhead the transition to Spaceland is the bridge corporation. It fits the definition of the corporation above, with one exception. Galambos developed his concept of the corporation by focusing on what would be the ideal business structure in freedom. But as you may have surmised, many aspects of its structure are illegal in Flatland, e.g., replacing employees with contractual associates, no hourly or annual wages, and no control of corporations by financial investors. Thus, he created the concept of the bridge corporation, a profit-seeking entity designed to be legal under Flatland laws and regulations yet based on Spaceland values and principles. The latter makes it resilient (anti-fragile) enough to survive the likely intensifying state coercion of the transition period. It is designed to operate in Flatland in the full light of day and not in a clandestine, underground way.

A bridge corporation is structured to operate in a manner legally acceptable to state bureaucrats. It is not unlike how the protagonist of Edgar Allen Poe's story "The Purloined Letter" hides the stolen documents right out on his desktop in plain view. Thus, we develop companies that will blaze the trail to Spaceland and the survival of our species in ways that do not raise the suspicions of coercive bureaucrats. Bridge corporations will provide essential services and generate enough taxable revenue to make them indispensable to the state, thus immune to interference. Without evading, but conforming to, current laws, bridge corporations will build ventures that can survive and prosper in today's coercive world and beyond.

The bridge corporation will do business in a way that accords with freedom to the degree possible. Keep in mind that freedom will not be attained overnight. It is an evolutionary, entrepreneurial process. If done competently, as high-level production increases, coercion will diminish. As production becomes more secure, the state will begin withering away.

In a free society, there's no market for state "services." Deregulated insurance companies in a competitive market would provide security, such as protection from violent criminals that states fail to provide. Private transportation companies would provide high-tech roads so advanced that few people, eventually no one, would suffer injury or death. Myriad entrepreneurs would create profit-seeking companies of all sizes and shapes seeking to satisfy customers in the market for therapies that repair injuries and cure or prevent diseases, including old age, all in a competitive market of doctors, nurses, hospitals, clinics, and preventive medical institutes. When we finally achieve civilizational escape velocity, bridge corporations will have evolved into normal Spaceland corporations.

No social institution is more important than the profit-seeking corporation. It is the only kind of business enterprise that can enter the *species* timescale. To achieve durability, it will focus on developing evolutionary sequences of products with the potential to grow and evolve without end. It will take entrepreneurs of unusual integrity, strength, and competence to create and run this new kind of company.

Are you ready for the adventure of a lifetime?

★   ★   ★

Recap

- The new business structure of Spaceland will function with two modes of compensation: the revenue share and the equity share.
  - Revenue share: Compensation that is a mutually negotiated percentage of gross revenue during a specified time.
  - Equity share: The total gross revenue minus all the expenses of a business during a specified time.
- In Flatland, the relationship between innovators and entrepreneurs is dysfunctional due to the win-lose attitude inherited from socialism. In Spaceland, they become natural allies. Entrepreneurs' profits derive from innovation, which makes them the primary customers for innovators' ideas.
- In Spaceland, innovators and contractual associates will be paid with revenue shares. Entrepreneurs will be compensated by equity shares. Entrepreneurs who take all the risks of managing the business receive 100 percent of the profit. The equity share is their only and total compensation.

- Revenue shares eliminate the inherent conflicts between employers and employees. With revenue shares, everyone in the networked enterprise works together to increase revenue, with the entrepreneur guiding the overall process toward consistently higher profits.

- Each person is paid for the value he creates for the business as determined by the entrepreneur(s) with whom he has contracted. This is an important component of justice. People should be paid according to what their efforts are worth to the one who's paying them. There is no other valid standard for determining compensation.

- In volitional science, there are no employers or employees. Today's employers will become tomorrow's buyers of services. Today's employees will become tomorrow's sellers of services. They are no longer in a master-slave relationship. They are independent suppliers in a win-win contractual relationship that encourages both parties to cooperate in pursuit of mutual profit.

- Sellers of services have more control over their destiny. They negotiate when and under what conditions they work. They become independent contractual associates. To earn more, they will guarantee the quality of their services and assume the risks and responsibilities accompanying independence.

- Certain market entities that exist in Flatland, such as clearinghouses, insurance companies, and corporations, will evolve from their current structures into more robust and lasting entities through entrepreneurial initiative.

10

The Path to a Spacefaring Civilization

These are the times that try men's souls. The summer soldier and the sunshine patriot will, in this crisis, shrink from the service of their country; but he that stands by it now, deserves the love and thanks of man and woman. Tyranny, like hell, is not easily conquered; yet we have this consolation with us, that the harder the conflict, the more glorious the triumph. What we obtain too cheap, we esteem too lightly: it is dearness only that gives every thing its value. Heaven knows how to put a proper price upon its goods; and it would be strange indeed if so celestial an article as FREEDOM should not be highly rated.
—Thomas Paine

NO SOCIETY OF VOLITIONAL BEINGS can expand indefinitely beyond its home planet until it implements absolute morality and its central principle of noncoercion, such that moral behavior becomes customary. At that point, it will reach civilizational escape velocity and become a cosmic civilization.

> **Cosmic civilization:** A society that has achieved a level of freedom sufficient to create an irreversible transformation into a spacefaring civilization.

A volitional species anywhere in the universe must adopt morality as its fundamental standard of behavior if it wishes to expand indefinitely into the cosmos. The alternative is to be overwhelmed by entropy and extinction. Without secure property rights, institutional coercion will undermine its ability to tap into natural energy flows, utilize them to enhance survival, and reuse or dissipate the resulting exhaust.

Necessary Steps to Freedom

I foresee two giant steps in humanity's immediate future: first, we become a spacefaring species; second, we develop biomedical science to the degree that we can to extend the healthy lifespan indefinitely. Ever since NASA reached the moon, state efforts to go beyond our planet have stagnated. We will leave this planet on the wings of profit-seeking companies such as Elon Musk's SpaceX, which has pioneered the private exploration of space. In 2022 and 2023, SpaceX launched more than 120 rockets and returned them to Earth. Musk said, "In order for us to have a future that's exciting and inspiring, it has to be one where we're a space-bearing civilization."[1] On the second front, in the last fifteen years, a myriad of entrepreneurs have founded start-up ventures focused on understanding the aging process and extending youthful longevity.

To achieve such wonders, we must develop a social system that dispenses with war and all forms of coercion and evolves into an expansive civilization impervious to collapse. Volitional science offers a blueprint for how to do this. If you think this is delusional or impossible, consider this: What law of nature does it violate? Furthermore, what is *your* alternative to the current world of political barbarism? Since we developed the ability to build weapons of mass destruction in a world of political states willing to deploy them, how can we guarantee they will never be used? It was the US military, not the Nazis, not the Russian or Chinese communists, that destroyed two Japanese cities with nuclear bombs. How can intelligent people believe in the necessity of political states that accept war as an acceptable tool of statecraft? Outside of volitional science, no one has a coherent answer to these questions.

We will not escape such a world by fighting or rebelling against it. Volitional science does not advocate sudden revolutionary change. Fighting tyranny will never achieve freedom. Volitional science rejects coercion as a means of accomplishing any positive goal. Political activism does not work. Innovators, entrepreneurs, and associated individuals cooperating in profit-seeking ventures produce all progress. That has always been the case. We can only create a civilization of freedom through a pragmatic entrepreneurial process. There are a vast number of potential ways forward. We need to unleash a new breed of entrepreneurs who will pioneer at least a few.

Volitional science offers a theory of the social domain with universal reach. It first defines individual action in universal terms (the first postulate) from which it derives the natural laws governing human interaction and cooperation. All possible actions can be divided into two classes, voluntary and coercive, which are demarcated by the boundary of property ownership. Markets emerge from voluntary actions. That's why they are so effective at delivering results that most people, by their actual choices, desire.

Political states are defined by their dependence on coercive interactions, which is why they always fail. Forcing someone to produce, or produce in a certain way, is called slavery. Slave societies are either primitive societies or once prosperous cultures that are devolving back toward destitution.

Markets are the nursery of progress. They are natural evolutionary systems governed by myriad autocatalytic feedback loops that regulate action at all levels toward production and prosperity. State agents employ top-down social engineering to force coercive constraints on market behavior. In contrast, free markets emerge bottom-up from voluntary interactions to support ongoing cooperation. Profit-seeking entrepreneurs operating in free markets provide everything that makes our lives more secure, convenient, and creative.

This raises a critical question: How do we convince people to respect property ownership without passing laws or imposing morality on them? It will not be done through a movement or a cause. Preaching, teaching, and hectoring do not work. Gaining acceptance of the new concept of morality will not involve educating the public or changing human nature. Most people aren't interested in science, moral philosophy, or great literature. Very few will pursue an understanding of scientific innovation. We will reach them by creating products and services that make their lives better and, through that process, instill moral behavior as a by-product.

The average American purchases the necessities of everyday life from supermarkets, pharmacies, and online stores. They don't steal them. Why? It's less costly and more profitable to buy them from a reliable company. Even in today's crime-ridden society, almost everyone prefers to buy and sell through voluntary means the things they believe will get them through the day and improve their lives. The principles of noncoercion and freedom will be introduced into modern culture as a by-product of the way Steve Jobs introduced the iPhone. Profit-seeking companies have always been the channel through which novel ideas have reached the public.

Absolute morality captures the ideals of "do no harm" and reciprocity in one principle. It has worked wherever it has been even partially implemented. The more the members of society respect property rights, the more that society exhibits the qualities we call civilized: low crime, diminishing violence, high prosperity, and flourishing artistic and scientific communities.

In Spaceland, in contrast with Flatland, there will be only one general rule governing individual action. A volitional being may pursue any moral action he wishes but may not pursue any action involving coercion. Such a standard will be maintained by market justice, of which compensation and restitution are two major components.

That an action is moral does not imply it is important, productive, or harmless. It may be exceedingly stupid. It may be harmful to the person undertaking it. In a free society, such actions have natural consequences the perpetrator will have to live with. The principle of natural justice means that people live with the consequences of their actions. In a cosmic civilization, people will not be forced to pay for the harmful consequences of someone else's actions. Everyone assumes responsibility for the risks deriving from their actions. Everyone will have skin in the game. That implies a civilization of optimal learning. People who are not protected from their failure will have the opportunity to learn and mature thereby. Some may even become wise.

Failure and Growth

Anyone who has lost money on an entrepreneurial venture knows that moral actions often fail. In a free market society, the consequences of failure are limited to the participants in the venture and no one else. But in Flatland, when a bank fails in the state-mandated financial system, its losses are imposed by the state on the entire population. Everyone suffers when a new law is passed, especially when measured by its long-term effects. That's because every new law applies to everyone and mandates more coercion backed by the threat of violence.

History is replete with failure, which would be bad news except for one redeeming quality of humans: we learn from our mistakes. However, cumulative learning is only possible in a culture of freedom. The reason is simple. Institutional coercion, whether religious or political, suppresses innovation, destroys information, and obstructs people from applying what they've learned to new ventures.

"One of the peculiar features of history is that empires are bad at innovation," Matt Ridley pointed out.

Though they have wealthy and educated elites, imperial regimes tend to preside over gradual declines in inventiveness, which contribute to their eventual undoing. The Egyptian, Persian, Roman, Byzantine, Han, Aztec, Inca, Hapsburg, Ming, Ottoman, Russian and British empires all bear this out. As time goes by and the central power ossifies, technology tends to stagnate, elites tend to resist novelty and funds get diverted into luxury, war or corruption, rather than enterprise.[2]

Politicians and bureaucrats offer to protect people from the consequences of their mistakes by paying them for failure, thus preventing them from learning from their errors. It is an anti-welfare system. States attack successful investors and entrepreneurs who produce the goods and services that provide a high standard of living. State agents seize producers' profits and give them to people who refuse to produce anything of value. Can you conceive of a more effective way to undermine and destroy a prosperous culture?

The physical and biological sciences continually produce knowledge that shows prior explanations to have been wrong. The Copernican heliocentric system replaced the Ptolemaic system when Copernicus's explanation was seen as better. Ptolemaic naked-eye astronomers were not acting immorally. In fact, they provided us with enormous value. They produced a thousand years of observational data that Copernicus and, later, Kepler used to create a more accurate description of the solar system. The reigning authorities acted immorally when they employed coercion to prevent these new ideas from spreading, thus obstructing further progress for several centuries. Yet today, societies use the same coercive tactics that have destroyed every culture since the Chaldean empire eight thousand years ago.

Every action is rational from the frame of reference of those undertaking it. No one pursues an action they think won't gain them what they're pursuing. A society that punishes people for making mistakes or tries to insulate them from the consequences of their failures is a society headed for catastrophe. In a civilization based on the norm of property rights, mistakes are not punished. Instead, error is quickly discovered, exposed, and publicized. The one who made the mistake will suffer a loss. That's the spur to improve. In freedom, people learn from mistakes. Without freedom, coercion suppresses knowledge and perpetuates ignorance.

Another way to view morality is as a search for general rules that will effectively foster and support widespread peaceful cooperation. We evolved as social beings because we discovered that working together in profit-seeking ventures enhanced our welfare more effectively than any other means.[3] Widespread, sustained cooperation can only arise in markets emerging from voluntary, noncoercive property exchanges.

Real-World Corroboration

West Berlin and East Berlin: As an eighteen-year-old student, I visited Berlin, an island of West Germany deep inside Communist East Germany. A section of the Berlin Wall ran through the middle of Berlin, dividing a city that for centuries had been one metropolis into two separate political jurisdictions. The socialist East German regime built the wall in 1961; they allowed no trade or travel between East and West.

When I arrived in Berlin in 1966, people who shared the same history, language, and ethnicity had been forced to live in two different social systems for almost two decades. West Berliners were refused entry to East Berlin, and East Berliners were shot if they tried to get into West Berlin.

West Germany was partially a market society based on a certain level of property rights. Profit-seeking companies provided most of the goods and services. East Germany was a fully Communist country where private property was strictly verboten. When both countries were born in the wake of World War II, their citizens had approximately the same level of per capita wealth.

West Germany established a market economy with little regulation during the first decades after the war. Ludwig Erhard, finance minister from 1949 to 1963, was a student of Austrian economics and understood the efficacy of free markets. In 1948, to the dismay of the head of the Allied occupying forces and without their permission, Erhard abolished price controls and rationing, thus allowing businesses to freely sell their goods to anyone at whatever price they could get. The West German economy took off in what became known as the "German Economic Miracle." Meanwhile, Communists imposed a state-run socialist economy in East Germany. Profit-seeking companies and private property were strictly illegal. Eighteen years later, I saw the results.

The city of West Berlin was a capitalist island walled off on all sides by socialist East Germany, 150 kilometers from the West German border. Yet, West Berlin was a booming modern city bustling with activity. It was a riot of color, a city full of neon signs and modern stores buzzing with young people on the make.

I was there in 1966 during a period of détente in the Cold War. It was one of the few periods during which Westerners could visit East Berlin under limited conditions. I got the appropriate visa, hopped on the subway, and emerged in East Berlin to an appalling sight. Compared to the colorful swirl of West Berlin, East Berlin was a dreary, colorless place painted in different shades of gray. It was like a black-and-white movie. The buildings were shabby, dilapidated, and rundown. There were few lights or anything requiring electricity. The few stores and cafés I found were filthy and permeated with foul smells. The service was nonexistent. There was no life, no bustle, no joy. The contrast with West Berlin was shocking. If you suspect my impressions were ideologically tainted in favor of West Berlin, you'd be wrong. As a young student, I was a left-wing, anti-capitalist idiot biased in favor of socialism.

The only way back into West Berlin was through the notorious Checkpoint Charlie near the Brandenburg Gate. To get there, I had to pass through a bizarre series of stern, heavily armed East German border guards. Barbed wire was every-where. Once I made it past the heavily armed document checkers, I began trotting toward a large African American US soldier standing at the crossing point into West Berlin. He suddenly shouted, "Stop right where you are!" His tone was fierce. I stopped, scared out of my wits. "Now, walk slowly toward me with your hands out from your side."

When I reached the gate, the soldier's scowl became a broad grin. He shook my hand and said, "I didn't want you to get shot, buddy. They shoot anyone running toward the wall. There's nothing we can do until you cross the border."

Hong Kong and Communist China: Germany was one of three similar Orwellian experiments during the same period; the other two were Hong Kong versus Communist China and South Korea versus North Korea. The results match those of Germany. People of a single nation, culture, and language were forced into two separate countries, one relatively capitalist and the other socialist. At the start of the "experiment," each society had around the same level of per capita wealth. The more capitalist society always left the socialist system in the dust by any measure of health and wealth.

After the Communists took over mainland China, Hong Kong was a miserable place for most of its citizens. The initial flow of refugees lived in temporary dwellings the government had thrown up to house them. They were one-room cells in a multistory building open in the front: one family, one room. The fact that people would accept such miserable living quarters testified to the intensity of their desire to leave Red China.

When I visited Hong Kong in 1981, what I saw was far beyond what I expected. Most taxicabs were the latest Mercedes-Benz models. The city was alive with entrepreneurial moxie. One could feel the energy in its hustling populace. Its income tax was a flat 15 percent. There were no customs duties, tariffs, or sales taxes. Goods flowed freely in and out of its bustling ports. It featured some of the finest hotels in the world. The communist regime just across the border from Kowloon allowed no one to enter mainland China. No one wanted to. It was a sea of poverty and a virtual prison from which one might never return. Very few mainland Chinese were allowed to visit Hong Kong while it was a British colony. Many escaped to its relative freedom, but many drowned or were killed by communist border guards trying to escape.

By 1990, Hong Kong, a small island with virtually no natural resources except the minds of its people, a justice system based on English common law property rights, and the lowest taxes in the world, had developed a level of per capita wealth greater than that of the United States.[4] Meanwhile, in the same decades during which Hong Kong became the wealthiest society on Earth on a per capita basis, more than fifty million people starved to death in Communist China, a country with a huge land mass and bounteous natural resources.

South Korea and North Korea: In 1992, I visited Panmunjom in the demilitarized zone between the two Koreas. I was warned ahead of time that armed North Korean guards might shoot me if I looked them in the eye. North Koreans, except for the political and military leadership and their soldiers, were starving to death. At the same time, Seoul, South Korea, was a city of ten million well-fed people moving briskly about in pursuit of personal goals. I could feel the thrum of energy as I wandered around the city. While there, my hosts introduced me to a creative arts scene that has made some of the finest movies in the world.[5] I visited technology companies that produced advanced electronic goods from state-of-the-art factories.

Forty years earlier, South Korea was one of the poorest countries on the planet. North Korea still is. All it produces are weapons of mass destruction, huge pageants of goose-stepping drones, and mass starvation. Today, South Korea is home to a booming private economy making some of the world's most advanced machinery, transport systems, ocean-going commercial vessels, huge offshore oil rigs, and sophisticated technical devices such as laptop computers and mobile phones. Socialist North Korea remains one of the most destitute countries on Earth. Of course, its Dear Leader and his associates drive around in expensive cars and enjoy American movies, fine clothes, books, food, and alcohol forbidden to the ordinary people of North Korea.

If you build a wall around your country and shoot anyone who tries to escape, you've built a prison, not a country.

Stabilized Durable Growth

Stabilized Durable Growth: The condition that signals a society has irreversibly transformed into a cosmic spacefaring civilization. It is growth that, due to internal market controls, cannot blow up and collapse.

To develop the healthy cultural evolution necessary for survival, a volitional species needs the stable context of a social structure governed by the norms of property rights. Such norms provide the context for creative activity that is the sole source of scientific, technical, and entrepreneurial progress. A civilization where one's power derives not from coercion but from serving others and is dispersed via property rights fosters robust markets in ideas, artistic works, technologies, and products that make prosperity and, thus, survival possible.

Life emerged from an evolutionary process that figured out how to temporarily overcome the universal flow toward randomness and entropy in a local area. Life did so by exploiting the emergent phenomenon of dynamic biochemical stability. To survive, we must develop another kind of stability: *stabilized durable growth*. It can only be achieved in a society whose members respect property ownership, including the ownership of intellectual property. That means a civilization in which it is the custom to adhere to the principle that an owner controls all property he has created or acquired in voluntary exchange. That is the governing rule of markets. It is a rule that most people voluntarily adhere to as they go about their daily lives.

The exceptions are politicians and bureaucrats, who regularly violate property boundaries. It is a job requirement that they continually coerce their citizens. But every act of coercion adds to entropy's destructive forces in the volitional world. Without market incentives to continually create and produce higher-quality property, the relentless forces of disintegration and disorder—physical, biological, and political—will overwhelm us as they have every past civilization.

Only through a civilization that supports innovation, technological advances, and vigorous entrepreneurial production can we protect ourselves from the physical forces of disintegration, the biological forces of disease and aging, and the ignorant forces of political and religious coercion. In the biological and volitional worlds, the cost of stupidity is extinction.

Innovators create the ideas that become knowledge. Entrepreneurs create new products and services. Artists create new works of art. Scientific innovators create new explanations and integrate their discoveries with the cumulative knowledge of past innovators. The most consequential innovators create new hypotheses that become general theories with reach and depth, as other scientists, inventors, and entrepreneurs find these explanations valuable.

Volitional science holds that cultural evolution in the form of scientific and technological progress will sooner or later provide us with the tools to control biological evolution and, someday, in the distant future, enable us to alter the basic structure of the physical universe if we so choose. The development of knowledge is cumulative and subject to periods of sudden exponential growth. Its outcomes are unpredictable because its progressive development depends on innovation. When we might develop such potent capabilities is unknowable. Our challenge is to survive the current age of barbarism and develop a civilization that can make such things possible.

Intergalactic Trade

All intelligent beings in contact with each other can enter mutually profitable exchange relationships. A highly advanced civilization will understand Ricardo's law of association, which says it's always more profitable for people from an advanced culture to enter peaceful trading relationships with less educated, less wealthy individuals from primitive cultures.

Members of an advanced alien civilization that has expanded far beyond its original home would consider it anathema to kill or enslave members of a more primitive society. Yet, most people assume that encounters with alien civilizations will be hostile. That's not only absurd, it's impossible. If you don't think so, you've been exposed to too much atavistic science fiction about wars in outer space.

There will never be an interstellar or intergalactic war. Most science fiction is based on crude Manichaean narratives of war and all manner of coercive intrigue. It's the good guys from Earth fighting off attacks from hostile aliens. But as I have explained, for any species of volitional beings to enter upon a sustained expansion beyond their original home, they must have discovered and implemented absolute morality. That means it would be their custom to respect an owner's property as the basis of all interactions with other volitional beings.

Civilizations far in advance of our own will understand the disutility of slavery and war. Otherwise, they could not have developed their own form of capitalism, the only social structure that can support the development of the advanced technology necessary to expand into the cosmos indefinitely.

TV shows and movies like *Star Trek* or *Star Wars* turn the grand adventure of exploring the cosmos into a puerile nightmare of militaristic empires engaging in endless wars. In 1898, H. G. Wells wrote a popular novel, *War of the Worlds*, about giant beings from Mars attacking Earth. These are all complete fantasies. Such things will never happen. With few exceptions, these shows even get the physical science wrong. Even "hard" science fiction features political systems and war.

The concept of hostile aliens attacking humans is ridiculous. A civilization so advanced it could easily overwhelm us would never have to fight a war. To attain such an advanced level of science and technology as to travel beyond their home planet, they would have solved the problem of institutional coercion, the problem any intelligent species must eventually resolve if it is to survive and prosper. It is the same challenge we face today. Our forebears developed physical science over the preceding three millennia to the point that we've produced the technology to destroy ourselves. But we have not until now developed a social science to the degree that would explain how we can prevent such a disaster.

Any civilization that can expand into the cosmos will have gone through that crisis. They will have figured out how to transcend the political state long ago. If we act in a hostile manner toward them, they will have technologies to defend themselves against such trivial pests. War with such a civilization is absurd. If anything, they would be curious about us and want to interact with us. They might view us as foolish children. They would certainly not kill us. It's impossible to predict the specifics of such future encounters except in the general terms discussed above.

Even if they had developed advanced forms of superintelligence, aliens from an advanced capitalist world would still use reason and logic to communicate with us. They will have no desire to conquer or enslave us. We will pose no threat to them, and they will pose no threat to us. If anything, they would view us as a primitive society that they might help transition into a civilization as peaceful, innovative, and sophisticated as theirs. If they thought they could profit from interacting with us, they would trade and associate with us. If we were still immersed in a barbaric political culture, they would probably stay far, far away.

In his book *The Beginning of Infinity*, physicist David Deutsch wrote, "People are the most significant entities in the cosmic scheme of things. They are not 'supported' by their environments but support themselves by creating knowledge. Once they have suitable knowledge (essentially, the knowledge of the Enlightenment), they can spark unlimited progress."

I couldn't agree more. Volitional science is a field of empirical knowledge rooted in the Enlightenment. It offers a blueprint for "unlimited further progress" informed by great thinkers of the past and the future. It only needs to be developed further and implemented by today's visionary innovators and entrepreneurs if we are to become a spacefaring civilization.

★ ★ ★

Recap

- Cosmic civilization: A society that has reached a level of freedom sufficient to create an irreversible transformation into a spacefaring civilization.

- Humanity has two giant advances to anticipate. Both will be vastly accelerated by the achievement of the cosmic civilization we call Spaceland. First, we will become a spacefaring species; second, we will indefinitely extend the healthy human lifespan. We may be close to some form of superintelligence, which would accelerate the achievement of both. These are achievable because neither violates a law of nature.

- In a spacefaring civilization, any action involving coercion is immoral and forbidden. Such a standard will be maintained by noncoercive market justice, of which compensation and restitution are two major components.

- Morality is a search for general rules of conduct that will effectively support the broadest system of peaceful cooperation. It is the most effective means of achieving what most people seek. We evolved as social beings because we discovered that working together in voluntary cooperation enhances our welfare and supports benevolent progress more effectively than any other means. By trial and error over time, we have discovered that cooperation becomes most effective in profit-seeking ventures.

- Three Orwellian experiments in the twentieth century showed a side-by-side comparison of capitalist and socialist societies: West Berlin versus East Berlin, Hong Kong versus Communist China, and South Korea versus North Korea. The more capitalist society has always left the socialist system in the dust by any measure of health and wealth.

- How do we convince people to act morally without passing laws or imposing morality on them? We create products and services that make their lives better and instill moral behavior as a by-product.

- Volitional science holds that cultural evolution in the form of scientific and technological progress will provide us with the tools to control biological evolution and alter the structure of the universe if we choose.

- There will never be an interstellar war. Highly advanced civilizations know it's always more profitable for an advanced culture to enter a peaceful trading relationship with more primitive ones than to kill or enslave its members. Furthermore, the structure of the universe will not allow an intelligent (volitional) species to expand beyond its original home until it has developed a civilization in which noncoercive (moral) interactions have become customary.

GLOSSARY

These definitions reflect how the words are used in volitional science and may not conform to the standard dictionary definitions.

Absolute: That which is independent of arbitrary standards of determination. It is that which is the same for all observers.

> **Absolute morality:** The minimal set of rules governing behavior a volitional species must adopt as customary for its civilization to survive and prosper indefinitely. It can be stated in one principle: Never interfere with an owner's control of his property without his consent. Put positively: all actions that involve zero coercion are moral.

Anchor Point of History chart: A historical snapshot of who created our modern order of knowledge and how it occurred. Isaac Newton is the anchor point of our history.

ARD (Automatic Remoteness Dilution): An idea or invention is released to the market for anyone to use under a licensing agreement with two terms: noncoercive usage and a positive non-zero royalty. If licensees adhere to the two terms, they may determine how they will apply the idea and how much they will pay for it.

Axiom of Action: "It is an attempt to substitute a more satisfactory state of affairs for a less satisfactory one. We call such a willfully induced alteration an exchange. A less desirable condition is bartered for one more desirable." (Ludwig von Mises)

Bad: The opposite of good. It is anything people prefer to avoid. What someone considers bad is relative to that person alone.

Bridge corporation: A business structure designed to bridge the gap between the non-freedom of Flatland and the freedom of Spaceland.

Bureaucracy: A department of a state claiming the legal right to interfere with an owner's property.

Capitalism: The societal order whose mechanism is capable of protecting all forms of property.

Civilization: A society where the prevailing commercial and personal customs derive from the principle of noncoercion. It is a society in which respect for property rights has become customary.

Cosmic civilization: A society that has reached a level of freedom sufficient to create an irreversible transformation into a spacefaring civilization.

Clearinghouse: A central institution comprised of an open-ended network of an unlimited number of profit-seeking companies that collects, maintains, and distributes information about who owns what for the mutual benefit of its members.

Coercion: Any attempted intentional interference with the property of an owner without the owner's permission or consent.

Communism: The abolition of private property.

Compensation: A financial payment made in exchange for value received.

Contract: An uncoerced agreement between two or more parties that governs their interaction concerning property they own or morally control.

Corporation: A contractual association of individuals structured to fulfill a mutually agreed proprietary purpose on a profit-seeking basis.

Crime: A successful act of coercion.

Critical juncture: The point when progress in the physical sciences has enabled the production of weapons of mass destruction while the lack of progress in the social sciences has not generated knowledge of how to prevent their use.

Entropy: A measure of the disorder, or what we perceive as randomness, of a closed system. Entropy always increases in the physical universe at large, which governs the fundamental directional flow of energy in the universe.

Epistemology: The branch of philosophy dealing with the limits and validity of knowledge.

Equity share: Compensation defined as gross revenue minus all the expenses of a business during a specified time. Equity shares are the only form of compensation suitable for an entrepreneur.

Fascism: A social system in which private individuals ostensibly own the means of production but are subject to the coercive control of state agents.

Flatland: Shorthand for today's world dominated by coercive political systems.

Force: Coercion effected through physical violence or the threat of physical violence.

Fraud: The use of deception to interfere with an owner's control over their property.

Freedom: The societal condition wherein each individual has 100 percent control over his property.

Golden Rule: There are two versions: "In all things, do unto others what you would have them do unto you" and "Do not do unto others what you would not want them to do to you."

Good: The subjective preference of a person. It is anything he chooses. What someone considers good is relative to that person alone.

Government: Any profit-seeking entity offering products and services to protect property to which customers may subscribe.

Gratitude: The acknowledgment, where due, for value received.

Happiness: The integrated totality of a person's preferences at any time. Happiness is subjective and, thus, relative to each person.

Immoral act: Any volitional act that involves coercion.

Importance: A measure of the total amount of people and property something or someone affects over time.

Injustice: A crime to which there is no recourse.

Interference: Any degree of control over an owner's property without the owner's permission or consent.

Justice: The elimination of injustice. Justice starts with the natural consequences that follow from any action.

Law of bureaucracy: Institutional coercion will always achieve results opposite to those intended.

Law of thermodynamics:

> **First law:** Energy cannot be created or destroyed; it can only be converted from one form to another.

Second law: A theory asserting all energy transformation of any kind will increase the entropy of the entire universe.

Liberty: The condition in which an individual has full control of his or her property.

Market: An open-ended system of social cooperation in which all transactions and interactions among people are noncoercive. Markets are systems enabling interactions the participants expect to be win-win.

Moral act: Any volitional act that is not coercive. A moral act entails no interference with an owner's property.

Morality: The class of volitional actions that are not immoral. It is the totality of possible or potential noncoercive actions.

Natural estate: The totality of all property that accrues to people during their lives and thereafter. It is the cumulative store and record in perpetuity of the achievements and property they have created.

NETCO (Natural Estate Trust Company): A company that will manage the estates of people during and after their lifetimes. It will develop market systems to identify the value of innovations in the early stages and place a speculative bet on them before they're applied on a large scale.

NRD (Negotiated Remoteness Dilution): A mechanism by which a creator releases his property for use under terms of a contract he or his agent negotiates with licensees.

Ownership: A person's right to exercise exclusive control over their physical body (primordial property) and the primary and secondary property they create, produce, or acquire in voluntary exchange. It is the total, permanent control of property on a moral basis.

Postulate: In volitional science, it is a universal description of human action and what motivates it. Saying it is universal means it applies to every possible action every volitional being could take anywhere in the universe.

First Postulate: Volitional beings act to pursue greater happiness. Happiness is subjective to each separate individual.

Second Postulate: All pursuits of happiness that do not involve coercion are equally valid.

Profit: Any increase in happiness pursued through moral actions. In entrepreneurial terms, it is a natural financial measure guiding organizations to use available resources efficiently to create products and services that improve life. Profit measures how effectively entrepreneurs or businesses provide value to others.

Property: A person's physical body and everything he creates or produces, whether tangible or intangible. Volitional science recognizes three kinds of property: primordial, primary, and secondary.

> **Primordial property (P0, pronounced "P-zero"):** A person's physical body, including his brain and neurological system. It is the unique biophysical system that supports a person's existence as a conscious, volitional being.

> **Primary property (P1):** The intangible derivatives of a person's physical body, including his mind. It includes beliefs, thoughts, ideas, actions, innovations, designs, songs, stories, and emotions.

> **Secondary property (P2):** The tangible derivatives of a person's actions, e.g., tables, chairs, airplanes, semiconductors, shoes, smartphones, etc. It is the tangible property a person creates or acquires in voluntary trade.

Revenue share: Compensation that is a mutually negotiated percentage of gross revenue during a specified time. It is a generalization of a royalty today.

Right: The authority accorded an owner by social convention to control his physical body and all tangible and intangible property he creates until he transfers that right, where possible, to someone else. The ownership of primary property cannot be transferred.

Satisfaction: A person's state of happiness at any moment. When we act, we are always—100 percent of the time—pursuing greater satisfaction. Some individuals may choose to undergo periods of hardship when in pursuit of longer-term goals.

Slavery: The control of a person's body and the work he produces without his permission or consent.

Socialism: A social system in which the state controls all the means of production.

Society: An association of people who interact to produce and exchange property.

Spaceland: Shorthand for a spacefaring civilization.

Stabilized durable growth: The condition that signals a society has irreversibly transformed into a cosmic spacefaring civilization. It is growth that, due to internal market controls, cannot blow up and collapse.

State: An organization that claims and exercises a legal monopoly of coercion within a specified territorial boundary. It is an apparatus of coercion accorded respectability or legitimacy by the public.

Stealing: Seizure of another's property without his permission or consent.

Taxation: A euphemism for massive, recurring theft carried out by a small group of people within a society with the tacit approval of most others.

Timescales of human achievement: The four timescales are *trivial, personal, species,* and *cosmic.*

Transaction: A voluntary exchange of property between people.

Transaction principle: Transactions result from the different values each party places on the property being exchanged.

Uniqueness corollary: No two people have identical value systems.

Universal: That which applies everywhere in the universe.

Value: The subjective weighting a person attaches to goods or preferences relative to all other goods or preferences. Values are relative to each person; there are no absolute values.

Volition: The ability to assess different courses of action and choose one based on the expectation of gain and avoidance of loss. It arises in intelligent beings who can choose to pursue survival and greater happiness.

> **Volitional action:** The phenomenon upon which volitional science is based. Every time volitional beings act, they choose what they think will be the most effective way to achieve greater happiness and satisfaction.

> **Volitional being:** A living organism composed of a hierarchy of physical (biochemical) systems that exhibits volitional action. Humans are volitional beings.

Volitional intelligence: The ability to acquire and use knowledge and reason to make choices in the pursuit of survival and happiness. It's the cognitive process by which people decide on and commit to a course of action they believe to be in their best interest.

Volitional science: A revolutionary approach using the scientific method adapted to the characteristics of the human domain to explain volitional beings and the social systems that arise from their interactions.

ENDNOTES

Preface

1   Galambos's associates were Alvin Lowi, Jr., Billy Robinson, Charles Estes, Peter Bos, and Jay Snelson.

2   In 1961, Galambos established the Free Enterprise Institute (FEI). His initial course was Course 100, Capitalism: The Key to Survival. He eventually taught courses on intellectual property, investments and insurance, financial planning, physics, and journalism, among others. "Andrew Joseph Galambos," Wikipedia, last modified June 27, 2024, https://en.wikipedia.org/wiki/Andrew_Joseph_Galambos.

Introduction

1   "Nuclear Weapons: Who Has What at a Glance," Arms Control Association, July 2024, https://www.armscontrol.org/factsheets/nuclear-weapons-who-has-what-glance.

Chapter 1

1   While I define *volition* such that animals do not possess it, that does not give humans the right to kill them willy-nilly. In fact, once Galambos's concept of universal morality becomes accepted, it will lead to a new reverence for life, including the life of the most primitive animals. For those who believe some animals are intelligent, let me clarify. Galambos created the concept of *volitional beings* but never defined it with due precision. I defined the category volitional beings arbitrarily because it seemed to fit reality and it allowed me to develop more useful explanations of humans and our social systems. I intentionally chose defining characteristics that excluded all other forms of life.

2   Eric J. Chaisson, *Cosmic Evolution: The Rise of Complexity in Nature* (Harvard University Press, 2002).

3   To avoid grammatical awkwardness, I will often use the singular "he" to represent an individual volitional being. Please know that when not referring to a specific individual but to the general category of volitional individuals, the "he" includes both women and men on equal terms.

4   Ludwig von Mises, "Mises's Introduction to *Theory and History*," Ludwig von Mises Institute, July 14, 2010, https://mises.org/mises-daily/mises-introduction-theory-and-history.

5   Carl Menger, *Principles of Economics* (originally published in 1871; Ludwig von Mises Institute, 2019), https://www.libertarianism.org/publications/essays/mengers-principles-economics-praise-causal-realism.

6   Adam Ferguson, *An Essay on the History of Civil Society* (originally published in 1767; Legare Street Press, 2022).

7   Harvey A. Silverglate, *Three Felonies a Day: How the Feds Target the Innocent* (Encounter Books, 2009).

8   "You cannot get something for nothing, nothing is free," is an expression of the first and second laws of thermodynamics in the volitional world.

9   Bernard Mandeville, *The Fable of the Bees or Private Vices, Public Benefits*, originally published in 1732, https://www.earlymoderntexts.com/assets/pdfs/mandeville17321.pdf.

10   Ferguson, *An Essay on the History of Civil Society*.

11   F. A. Hayek, "Competition as a Discovery Procedure," *Quarterly Journal of Austrian Economics* 5, no. 3 (Fall 2002), https://mises.org/quarterly-journal-austrian-economics/competition-discovery-procedure. [This is a translation from German of F. A. Hayek's "*Der Wettbewerb als Entdeckungsverfahren*," a 1968 lecture sponsored by the Institut für Weltwirtschaft at the University of Kiel. Translated by Marcellus S. Snow.]

12   David Deutsch, *The Beginning of Infinity: Explanations That Transform the World* (Penguin Books, Reprint edition 2012).

13   Friedrich A. Hayek, "The Use of Knowledge in Society," Econlib, accessed July 12, 2024, https://www.econlib.org/library/Essays/hykKnw.html.

14   Randy Alfred, "Feb. 22, 1857: Hertz Enters Cycle of Life," *Wired*, February 22, 2010, https://www.wired.com/2010/02/0222heinrich-hertz-born/#:~:text=Hertz%20regarded%20his%20discoveries%20as,But%20they%20are%20there.

15   "Heinrich Rudolf Hertz," Wayback Machine, http://web.archive.org/web/20090925102542/http://chem.ch.huji.ac.il/history/hertz.htm.

16   Galileo Galilei, *Dialogue Concerning the Two Chief World Systems: Ptolemaic and Copernican* (originally published in Florence in 1632; Modern Library, New edition 2001).

Chapter 2

1   *Britannica*, "Occam's Razor," last updated October 21, 2024, https://www.britannica.com/topic/Occams-razor.

2   The most important book ever published, Isaac Newton's *Principia Mathematica*, is the intellectual platform from which all modern science has since emerged. It begins with a section entitled "Definitions." In the first several pages, Newton gave precise definitions of eight fundamental terms of the discourse to follow. Then he spent several pages carefully analyzing his definitions and how they differ from the common usage of the same terms.

3   "Lysander Spooner," Online Library of Liberty, accessed July 1, 2024, https://oll.libertyfund.org/people/lysander-spooner.

4   For instance, politicians introduce price controls to make products cheaper, but that disincentivizes entrepreneurs producing the goods, resulting in lower profits, less production, and shortages instead of *price controls* leading to greater availability and lower cost. The term price controls is purposefully misleading. All such laws are the coercive control of people.

5   David Deutsch, *The Beginning of Infinity: Explanations That Transform the World* (Viking, 2011), 212.

6   Robert Higgs, "The State Is Too Dangerous to Tolerate," Mises Institute, July 28, 2013, https://mises.org/podcasts/mises-u-2013/state-too-dangerous-tolerate.

7   Higgs, "The State Is Too Dangerous to Tolerate."

8   Matt Ridley, *How Innovation Works: And Why It Flourishes in Freedom* (HarperCollins, 2020), 30.

9   Michael D. Gordin, "Lysenkoism," *Encyclopedia of the History of Science*, accessed July 16, 2024, https://ethos.lps.library.cmu.edu/article/id/560/.

10   Claude E. Shannon and Warren Weaver, *The Mathematical Theory of Communication* (University of Illinois Press, 16th printing, 1971).

Chapter 3
1   Henry Hazlitt, *The Foundations of Morality*, 3rd ed. (Foundation for Economic Education, 1998).

2   Arthur Eddington, *The Philosophy of Physical Science* (originally published in 1939; Minkowski Institute Press, 2021).

3   Thomas Hobbes, *Leviathan* (originally published in 1651; Penguin Classics, 2017).

4   Coercive actions often produce a short-term gain for the perpetrator. Except for one category of actions, the perpetrator suffers a far greater long-term loss. The exception is political coercion, which produces a short-term gain for bureaucrats, generals, and politicians who force the rest of us to eat the losses entailed.

5   The US Federal Register lists all federal rules and regulations. By the end of 2023, it was 90,402 pages. The Code of Federal Regulations is a list of all regulations foisted on Americans in addition to those in the Federal Register. By 2021, it contained 188,000 pages. US citizens and residents are expected to obey all of them.

6   Diogenes Laertius, *The Lives and Opinions of Eminent Philosophers* (Books 6–10) (Independently published, 2020).

7   Thales (624–546 BCE): "Avoid doing what you would blame others for doing."
      Confucius (551–479 BCE): "What you do not wish for yourself, do not do to others."
      Hillel (c. 90BC–10 CE): "That which is hateful to you, do not do to your fellow. That is the whole Torah; the rest is the explanation; go and learn."
      Thomas Hobbes (1588–1679): "Do not that to another which thou wouldst not have done to thyself."

8   When Galambos made this claim of universality, he acknowledged he was taking a risk. Humans are unable at this point in our history to corroborate that claim observationally. Nevertheless, it is no different from Newton's claim of universality for his concepts of motion, gravitation, and light before they could be observationally confirmed.

9   Joseph Spence, *Anecdotes, Observations and Characters, of Books and Men*, Vol. 1 (London: John Murray, Albemarle-Street, 1820), 158.

10   Rousseau's concept of the general will has been described thusly: "The general will corresponds to the set of choices made by all citizens, each truly expressing himself for the good of all and not for his own good." Try

to unpack the meaning of that sentence. How would a citizen disentangle choices made "for the good of all" from choices made "for his own good"? For several millennia most political theorists have claimed similar principles as the basis for whatever social structure they advocated.

Chapter 4

1   "Leibniz's Modal Metaphysics," *Stanford Encyclopedia of Philosophy*, May 23, 2008, revised February 8, 2013, https://plato.stanford.edu/entries/leibniz-modal/.

2   Edgar Iandivar, "The Almost Unknown Bet That Changed the History of Humanity," Neomano, June 27, 2020, https://neomano.com/en/the-almost-unknown-bet-that-change-the-history-of-humanity/.

3   Frédéric Bastiat, *What Is Seen and What Is Not Seen, or Political Economy in One Lesson* [1850], OLL, https://oll.libertyfund.org/pages/wswns.

4   "Independent Contractor Versus Employee," California Department of Industrial Relations, updated January 2023, https://www.dir.ca.gov/dlse/faq_independentcontractor.htm.

5   Nemanja Jovancic, "43 Steve Jobs Quotes on Business, Startups and Innovation," LeadQuizzes, October 19, 2018, https://www.leadquizzes.com/blog/steve-job-quotes/.

Chapter 5

1   *Britannica*, "Sadi Carnot," updated September 29, 2024, https://www.britannica.com/biography/Sadi-Carnot-French-scientist.

2   Arthur Stanley Eddington, *The Nature of the Physical World* (originally published in 1928; Kessinger Publishing, 2010).

3   The best hypothesis for how life arose on Earth around 3.8 to 4 billion years ago suggests with good evidence that it appeared in the environment around deep ocean hydrothermal vents using energy stored in the core of the Earth released into the ocean or atmosphere via oceanic thermal vents, volcanoes, earthquakes, etc.

4   "The process by which fatty acid micelles may form a vesicle is shown in this animation," US National Science Foundation, accessed July 24, 2024, https://www.nsf.gov/news/news_images.jsp?cntn_id=111652&org=NSF.

5   One of the major leaps during the birth of the first cells was the development of a barrier to separate the intracellular and extracellular environments. Membranes provide many advantages: (a) molecules for metabolic reactions are held together and are not lost by diffusion; therefore, the chance of chemical reactions is higher and more efficient; (b) internal molecules are not shared with neighbors, so that new advantageous molecules for new chemical pathways are not used by competitors, that is, "selfish evolution"; (c) a proper internal environment can be set to enhance chemical reactions and to counteract external environmental changes. From "The Origin of the Cell," Atlas of Plant and Animal Histology, accessed July 24, 2024, https://mmegias.webs.uvigo.es/02-english/5-celulas/1-origen_celula.php.

6   It has been hypothesized that our mitochondria emerged when a single-celled organism ate another such organism and the engorged organism not only remained intact but conveyed an advantage to the predator and thus became the energy-producing unit with its own boundary within the cells of complex organisms.

7   Eddington, *The Nature of the Physical World*.

8   Voltaire, *Letters on England* (originally published in 1733), The Project Gutenberg eBook, ed. Henry Morley, published April 22, 2005, https://www.gutenberg.org/files/2445/2445-h/2445-h.htm.

9   F. A. Hayek, "Why the Worst Get on Top," chapter 10 from *The Road to Serfdom*, Foundation for Economic Education, December 16, 2015, https://fee.org/resources/the-road-to-serfdom-chapter-10-why-the-worst-get-on-top/?gad_source=1&gbraid=0AAAAADkIVmeJ2VsMi70mHon02au-v5LqlF&gclid=CjwKCAjwnei0BhB-EiwAA2xuBu2XWVYasDt1uGSXlwSN-JMVZnkNZakcMMDm0ve27IWjITZFYTbeZ7BoCF-QQAvD_BwE.

10   H. L. Mencken, "Sham Battle," *Baltimore Evening Sun*, October 26, 1936.

Chapter 6

1   The analysis in this section depends on the work of Ludwig von Mises and Peter Boettke. The latter's lucid essay "Was Mises Right?" in his book *Living Economics: Yesterday, Today, and Tomorrow* helped me in understanding the nature of volition and volitional action. The entire chapter is an introduction to my integration of Mises's and Galambos's work with that of Raymond Tallis, Carl Menger, F. A. Hayek, and Jay Stuart Snelson.

2   Adam Smith, *The Wealth of Nations* (originally published in 1776; Independently reprinted, 2019).

3   Alex makes two pies. He spends four hours of equal effort making each pie. One is an apple pie made according to his grannie's favorite recipe. The other is made from cow manure and pig urine. He labels each pie honestly. Believing that value derives from labor, he charges the same for each pie. Which pie will sell first?

4   Carl Menger, *Principles of Economics* (originally published in 1871; Ludwig von Mises Institute, 2019).

5   Carl Menger, *Principles of Economics*.

6   Carl Menger, *Principles of Economics*.

7   Ludwig von Mises, *Human Action: A Treatise on Economics*, https://cdn.mises.org/Human%20Action_3.pdf.

8   Rudyard Kipling, *Just So Stories* (originally published in 1902). This is Kipling's collection of stories he made up and told his daughter when he put her to bed. She demanded he tell each one "just so," exactly as he had told it the previous time. In science and philosophy, a just-so story is an untestable narrative explanation for a cultural practice, a biological trait, or a particular behavior of humans or other animals. For such narratives to be useful as science, they must conform to the laws of nature as we know them. They must also accord with reason, observational reality, and logic.

9   Raymond Tallis, *Aping Mankind: Neuromania, Darwinitis and the Misrepresentation of Humanity* (Routledge, 2011); Raymond Tallis, *The Hand: A Philosophical Inquiry into Human Being* (Edinburgh University Press, 2003); Raymond Tallis, *The Knowing Animal: A Philosophical Inquiry into Knowledge and Truth* (Edinburgh University Press, 2004).

Chapter 7

1   Innovators face a far more difficult challenge than entrepreneurs in that they cannot adjust their products to the desires of the public. They must explain reality as they see it, even if it conflicts with the widely held views of their time. Innovators must cater to reality rather than the whims and desires of peers or customers. The history of important innovations is littered with narratives of independent thinkers who faced enormous resistance when they disclosed their new ideas. If Galileo had catered to his peers, he would have ceased pursuing an Archimedean approach to mechanics and gone back to using Aristotle's methods.

2   The ideas Newton developed influence today's culture far more than anyone else's. His physical body is dead but his once-in-a-millennium mind produced ideas that are not only still influencing everyone and supporting the infrastructure of civilization, but also demonstrating the power and importance of scientific innovation on the *species* and *cosmic* timeframes. People live on after death in our minds and hearts. Isaac Newton and Thomas Paine have taken up permanent residence in mine.

3   "What Is Austrian Economics?" Mises Institute, accessed August 1, 2024, https://mises.org/what-austrian-economics.

Chapter 8

1   Edwin Abbott, *Flatland: A Romance of Many Dimensions* (originally published in 1884; Independently reprinted, 2020).

Chapter 10

1   Julia Steers, "Elon Musk on Mars: 'It's a fixer-upper of a planet.'" *CBS Mornings*, September 21, 2012, https://www.cbsnews.com/news/elon-musk-on-mars-its-a-fixer-upper-of-a-planet/.

2   Matt Ridley, *How Innovation Works: And Why It Flourishes in Freedom* (HarperCollins, May 2020), 264.

3   Galambos defined *profit* as any increase in happiness pursued exclusively through moral action. As such, it includes financial profit but also far more, e.g., the pursuit of knowledge for its own sake.

4   For more details, read "The Hong Kong Experiment" by Milton Friedman: https://www.hoover.org/research/hong-kong-experiment.

5   The Korean film *Parasite* won the Palme d'Or at the Cannes Film Festival in 2019. The film also won an Oscar in 2020 for best picture, the first foreign language film to win that Oscar. Director Bong Joon-ho won the Oscar that year for best director.

BIBLIOGRAPHY

Bell, Eric Temple. *Men of Mathematics*. Simon & Schuster, 1937.

Boren, John Richard. *For Intellectual Property: The Property Ideas of Andrew J. Galambos*. Createspace, 2016.

Chaisson, Eric J. *Cosmic Evolution: The Rise of Complexity in Nature*. Harvard University Press, 2002.

Cheney, Margaret. *Tesla: Man Out of Time*. Touchstone, 2001.

Combs, Harry. *Kill Devil Hill: Discovering the Secret of the Wright Brothers*. Houghton Mifflin Harcourt, 1979.

Dawkins, Richard. *The Blind Watchmaker*. W. W. Norton & Company; Reissue edition, 2015.

Deutsch, David. *The Fabric of Reality*. Penguin Books, 1998.

Deutsch, David. *The Beginning of Infinity*. Penguin Books, 2012.

Eddington, Arthur. *The Nature of the Physical World*. Kessinger Publishing, 2010.

Eddington, Arthur. *The Philosophy of Physical Science*. Minkowski Institute Press, 2021.

Einstein, Albert. *The World as I See It*. General Press, 2018.

Friedman, Milton. *Capitalism and Freedom*. University of Chicago Press, 1968.

Galambos, Andrew J. *Sic Itur Ad Astra*. The Free Enterprise Institute, 1998.

Galambos, Andrew J. *V:50: The Basic Course of the Volitional Sciences: 3-Session Introduction*. Independently published, 2023.

Galambos, Andrew J. *Course V-201: The Theory of Primary Property*. The Liberal Institute of Natural Science and Technology.

Galilei, Galileo. *Dialogue Concerning the Two Chief World Systems*. University of California Press, 2023.

Hayek, F. A. *The Constitution of Liberty*. University of Chicago Press, 1960.

Hayek, F. A. *Individualism and Economic Order*. University of Chicago Press, 1969.

Hayek, F. A. *The Road to Serfdom*. University of Chicago Press, 2007.

Hazelgrove, William. *Wright Brothers, Wrong Story: How Wilbur Wright Solved the Problem of Manned Flight*. Prometheus, 2018.

Hazlitt, Henry. *The Foundations of Morality*. Foundation for Economic Education; 3rd edition, 1998.

Higgs, Robert. *Crisis and Leviathan: Critical Episodes in the Growth of American Government*. Oxford University Press, 1987.

Hirshfeld, Alan. *Eureka Man: The Life and Legacy of Archimedes*. Walker Books, 2010.

Hobbes, Thomas. *Leviathan*. Penguin Classics, 2017.

Isaacson, Walter. *Einstein: His Life and Universe*. Simon & Schuster, 2007.

Keynes, John Maynard. *The General Theory of Employment, Interest, and Money*. Macmillan; 12th edition, 1960.

Mandeville, Bernard. *The Fable of the Bees*. Penguin Classics, 1989.

Menger, Carl. *Principles of Economics*. Ludwig von Mises Institute, 2019.

Nelson, Craig. *Thomas Paine: Enlightenment, Revolution, and the Birth of Modern Nations*. Penguin Publishing Group, 2007.

Newton, Isaac. *The Principia: Mathematical Principles of Natural Philosophy*. Translated by I. Bernard Cohen and Anne Whitman. University of California Press, 2016.

Paine, Thomas. *Collected Writings: Common Sense, The Crisis, Rights of Man, Age of Reason, Pamphlets, Articles & Letters*. Library of America, 1995.

Pinker, Steven. *Enlightenment Now: The Case for Reason, Science, Humanism, and Progress*. Penguin Books, 2019.

Popper, Karl R. *The Open Society and Its Enemies*. Princeton University Press, 2020.

Popper, Karl R. *Objective Knowledge: An Evolutionary Approach*. Oxford University Press; Revised edition, 1972.

Rhodes, Richard. *The Making of the Atomic Bomb*. Simon & Schuster, 1987.

Ricardo, David. *Principles of Political Economy and Taxation*. Dover Publications, 2004.

Ridley, Matt. *The Evolution of Everything: How New Ideas Emerge*. HarperCollins, 2015.

Ridley, Matt. *The Rational Optimist: How Prosperity Evolves*. HarperCollins, 2010.

Rothbard, Murray N. *Man, Economy, and State with Power and Market*. Ludwig von Mises Institute, 2011.

Rowland, Ingrid D. *Giordano Bruno: Philosopher/Heretic.* University of Chicago Press, 2009.

Seifer, Marc J. *Wizard: The Life and Times of Nikola Tesla.* Citadel Press, 2011.

Shannon, Claude E. and Warren Weaver. *The Mathematical Theory of Communication.* University of Illinois Press; 16th printing, 1971.

Silverglate, Harvey A. *Three Felonies a Day: How the Feds Target the Innocent.* Encounter Books, 2009.

Smith, Adam. *The Wealth of Nations.* Independently reprinted, 2019.

Snelson, Jay Stuart. *Taming the Violence of Faith: Win-Win Solutions for Our World in Crisis.* CreateSpace, 2012.

Snelson, Jay Stuart. *V-50: An Introduction to Volitional Science.* The Free Enterprise Institute. Independently published, 2023.

Tallis, Raymond. *Aping Mankind: Neuromania, Darwinitis and the Misrepresentation of Humanity.* Routledge, 2011.

Thompson, Morton. *The Cry and the Covenant.* Rare Treasures Press, 2024.

Von Mises, Ludwig. *Human Action: A Treatise on Economics.* Yale University Press, 2010.

Von Mises, Ludwig. *Theory and History: An Interpretation of Social and Economic Evolution.* Ludwig von Mises Institute; 2nd edition, 2007.

Von Mises, Ludwig. *The Ultimate Foundation of Economic Science: An Essay on Method.* D. Van Nostrand & Company, 1962.

Westfall, Richard S. *Never at Rest: A Biography of Isaac Newton.* Cambridge University Press, 1983.

White, Michael. *The Pope and the Heretic: The True Story of Giordano Bruno, the Man Who Dared to Defy the Roman Inquisition.* Harper Perennial, 2003.

ABOUT THE AUTHOR

John Deming

The intellectual odyssey that has consumed my life began on a porch in Pass Christian, Mississippi, in 1954. My father and I were each reading a book when he turned to me and said, "John, the most important thing a man can do is pursue knowledge for its own sake." I adored my father, so that sentence seared itself into my mind and became the guiding principle of my life.

It led me to begin sorting out what is important to know and what is not. In my pursuit of "ultimate truth," I discovered there is no such thing. After pursuing various pathways that initially looked promising, I stumbled upon physics and free market economic theory and found the subjects I would spend the rest of my life pursuing. Around that time, two friends, Evan Root and John Fountain, introduced me to the greatest instructor I could have ever hoped for in both subjects: astrophysicist Andrew J. Galambos. Starting at twenty-four, I spent the next five years as Galambos's student.

After studying with Galambos at his institute, I pursued an autodidactic self-education in three principal subjects: (1) scientific epistemology, (2) the historical development of social theory in Western culture, and (3) the history of science and scientific innovation from Thales and Pythagoras in sixth century BCE Greece to the present including the twentieth-century revolutions in relativity and quantum physics.

It is my hope that writing this book (and others to follow) will stimulate a deeper interest in Galambos's work and that of his associates, such as Jay Snelson and Alvin Lowi, Jr. My further goal is for his theories to gain traction in the world of technological entrepreneurship. For it is entrepreneurs and real scientists who will build the cosmic civilization of the future.

ABOUT THE EDITOR

Mike Hamel

I grew up in Colorado and did a bit of traveling before becoming the editor of INTEREST magazine in Chicago. In 1996, I moved back to Colorado Springs and started my career as a freelance writer. Since then, I've written everything from blog posts and web pages to magazine articles and anthologies. Along the way, I interviewed over 100 entrepreneurs and leaders for a series of books on entrepreneurship.

In the last twenty-eight years, I've authored or substantially edited over forty books on topics as wide-ranging as business, finance, political theory, healthcare, cancer, nonprofits, and religion. These include twenty books for children and young adults. Before working with John on this book, I did three other books on economics and social theory: *Entrepreneurial Communities: An Alternative to the State*, *Spencer MacCallum: A Man Beyond His Time*, and *Alvin Lowi, Jr: American Polymath*.

My wife, Cindy, and I still live in the shadow of Pikes Peak, surrounded by a gaggle of kids and grandkids. You can learn more about me on Amazon.

www.ingramcontent.com/pod-product-compliance
Lightning Source LLC
Chambersburg PA
CBHW052123270326
41930CB00012B/2737